Henry Coppée

Songs of Praise and Poems of Devotion

In the Christian Centuries

Henry Coppée

Songs of Praise and Poems of Devotion
In the Christian Centuries

ISBN/EAN: 9783337180836

Printed in Europe, USA, Canada, Australia, Japan

Cover: Foto ©Thomas Meinert / pixelio.de

More available books at **www.hansebooks.com**

SONGS OF PRAISE

AND

POEMS OF DEVOTION

IN THE CHRISTIAN CENTURIES.

WITH AN INTRODUCTION

By HENRY COPPÉE,

PROFESSOR OF ENGLISH LITERATURE IN THE UNIVERSITY OF PENNSYLVANIA.

ELEGANTLY ILLUSTRATED

WITH SIXTY STEEL ENGRAVINGS EXECUTED IN THE FIRST STYLE OF THE ART.

PHILADELPHIA:

PUBLISHED BY E. H. BUTLER & CO.

1872.

CONTENTS.

4 CONTENTS.

6   CONTENTS.

☞ The Singers, "God's Acre," and "Resignation," by Professor Longfellow, are published in this volume with the consent of MESSRS. TICKNOR & FIELDS.

LIST OF ILLUSTRATIONS.

INTRODUCTION.

WITHOUT intending to present an essay on Hymnology, I desire to offer a few explanatory remarks as to the volume now offered to the public, and the vast field, always white to the harvest, from which I have gleaned my little sheaves.

More than two years ago, a clerical friend, of rare culture and delicate taste,—who, moreover, always delights in sharing newly-discovered beauties with his friends and fellow-scholars,—brought to me a copy of the British edition of Neale's Hymns of the Eastern Church. We read it through with great delight in one happy evening. I had known Dr. Neale as the translator and collector of the Latin Mediæval Hymns, but I had not before seen this little book; and although, doubtless, it is known to many students of hymnology, I found, in showing them to numerous friends, that no one had seen them: they have not, to my knowledge, been republished in America.

Preceded by a learned introduction on Greek Christian poetry, the hymns are chronologically arranged, and a short account is presented of each author and his age. They begin with the fifth century, represented by St. Anatolius. I have not seen the originals; but if the translations do them no more than justice, they are beautiful: if, as is almost always the case, there are vernacular beauties which cannot be rendered in another tongue, too much cannot be said in their praise. But, considered simply as English poems, the translations are admirable: the language is simple, and the expression concentrated. The original rhythm is as far as possible retained, and thus to the energy of the Greek is added the pleasant ramble of the old English ballad. Of this the reader may judge by referring to almost any one of them. Take, for example, the "God of God," beginning,—

> "Fierce was the wild billow."

or those beginning,—

> "Art thou weary, art thou languid?"

and

> "Safe home, safe home in port."

Some of them rise to an epic grandeur, as, for example, that of St. Joseph of the Studium, of which the first line is,—

> "Stars of the morning, so gloriously bright!"

Ranging over the Christian Year, called by a clerical writer "the Zodiac of the Church," varied as they are in form, subject, and historic period, and yet catholic in tone, teaching, and spirit, they serve to show us of the modern age how the holy souls in all the centuries of Christianity, giving devout utterance in "psalms and hymns and spiritual songs," have made the same "melody in their hearts unto the Lord," so that when brought into our own speech we at once make them our own; we sing their songs as if we had always known them, and thank God for His goodness in their own beautiful words, which exemplify "diversities of gifts, but the same Spirit."

My first intention was merely to propose the reprinting of this little volume, that other Christian men and women should share the pleasure which I had experienced; but, upon even a cursory examination of the hymnals and modern collections in my possession, I found large space for a new volume of Songs of Praise, in which Neale's Eastern Hymns might be embodied, and other rare and beautiful Christian utterances presented.

And as the gift-days were coming, in commemoration of that greatest Gift of God to man, it was thought proper to prepare the book as a presentation-volume, by adorning the anthology of sacred poetry with the rare flowers of pictorial art. The result is this truly beautiful volume,—a Christmas chant to the new-born King in which the glorious diapason is sounded by Christian saints in all ages, without one discord to mar the catholic harmony. Thus much to avoid misunderstanding as to the character of the volume. It is not a general hymnal, but a choice collection of a few beautiful and not common hymns.

A hymnal proposing to present a historical picture of all the curious changes in Christian hymnology is, indeed, very much needed; but it would be a work of immense labor, demanding great erudition. It would clearly mark the great hymnic periods in the history of the Church, and the causes which produced them. It would show why the Western Church was still desti-tute of such songs in worship, while the Eastern Church had long used them, not only in her solemn services, but in the mouths of her children by the hearth-stone and in the harvest-field. It would take us back to St. Jerome at the monastery of Bethlehem, and to his great contemporary, Gregory of Nazianzen, who, doubtless, in their four years' residence together, discussed and promoted this great element of worship. It would inform us of the circumstances which in the fourth century spread these songs of praise throughout the world.

The history in such a hymnal would be rich and varied. Great occasions, great enlargements of mind, counsels and convocations, reforms general and national, have created a demand; and poets have sprung up from all ranks of life to supply the deficiency.

To the Fourth Council of Toledo, A. D. 633, is due the honor of having enacted that hymns should be used throughout the Western Church in public worship. When this was done, it was found that those of the Eastern Church were not easily translated, and that the West must prepare its own. Then emperors, kings, and popes vied with each other in this holy task. Charlemagne thought himself honored in composing hymns, and the churchmen, from pope to deacon, were prolific of sacred poetry. Popes like Innocent III., and bishops like Hilary of Poictiers, paid their tributes in beautiful verses; and St. Ambrose instituted choral singing in that Cathedral of Milan which was in after-days to become one of the wonders of Europe.

Thus were produced such poems as the *Te Deum*, the *Dies Iræ*, and the *Stabat Mater*. The Church in all ages since has embodied such strains in her holiest services, and thus has called upon old Judaism, which looked for Christ, and classic oracle, which groped for light, to acknowledge the might of Him who was at once King of the Jews and King of kings,

" Teste David cum Sybilla,"

Deep calling unto Deep in the soul of man, in all times and in all languages.

In such a hymnal, the increase and improvement of church *music* would be set forth, as a powerful instrument in awakening devotion. We should see how rhyming Latin conquered the ancient classic metres, and for a thousand years played an important part in the worship of God. These Latin hymns, ranging over this immense period, and the work of many gifted writers, were indeed encrusted with errors afterwards established by ecclesiastical edict; but underlying these were all the great truths of Christianity, expressed in fervid language, and shining through the gloom like diamonds in the dark mine.

Leo X., the unconscious instrument of the Reformation by his sale of indulgences for the building of St. Peter's, here also committed a fatal error for his cause. He frowned upon the rhymes and measures, and favored a return to the classic metres; but he could not curb the tide. The hymns, and the manner in which they were presented, had met with universal favor, and no papal denunciation could consign them to oblivion. But they are not to be tried by the standards of the Reformation, which, properly searching for their faults, foolishly ignored their beauties. Many of them are narrative; not a few are legendary, and even fabulous; some are turgid and obscure, like the *Pange lingua gloriosa* and the *Vexilla Regis;* but not a few, like the *Dies Iræ,* are of unrivalled grandeur.

The principal collection of the Latin hymns is found in the *Roman Breviary.* There had been many breviaries or divine offices for the canonical hours; but these, like the Uses in the reformed Anglican Church, were different for different localities. The Council of Trent, which established the doctrines of the Roman Catholic Church, likewise set forth a Breviary for universal adoption. This was slightly altered by Popes Clement VIII. and Urban VIII., who thus established the present Breviary. The French clergy, with a freedom which has always marked the French Church, altered and rearranged this, to constitute what is known as the Paris Breviary. In these is to be found the wealth of Latin hymns; and to them all collectors of the best Christian poetry must always go.

With the coming of the Reformation the Latin hymns, already coldly regarded by the pope, fell into temporary disrepute. Not only was there the natural prejudice of the reformers against the language in which they were written, and against the errors which they contained, but the great awakening seemed to

4

demand new poems and collections; and each nation called for the best in its own vernacular. Hence there have occurred hymnic periods from that time to our own; and hymns often not as good have replaced the old hymns which for so many centuries had given rapture to the cells of hermits and monks, had been sung by missionaries in primeval forests, and had been uttered with the last breath of dying saints.

We cannot pause even to indicate these periods. In the Elizabethan age occur the names of Crashaw, Herbert, Vaughn, and Wither; and Luther's noble psalm-book marks such an awakening in Germany. A later period produced the exquisite paraphrases of Addison; and Watts poured forth his devout spirit in a large volume of those sententious verses which, notwithstanding their faults of diction and their theological obscurities, still wing the devotions of millions, on Sundays and working-days alike, throughout the world.

It is no part of our purpose to refer to the hymn-writers and denominational hymn-books which have been produced since. In most cases they have been the efforts of men to supply a need; and, although they have failed in the perfect accomplishment, they have enriched the language and the Church with most grateful additions to its hymnic literature. Such were the collections of Sternhold and Hopkins, and of Tate and Brady: such were the efforts of the Wesleys, Montgomery, and Cowper.

But in every case the writers, following the dictates of a special creed, have presented their own views; and the collectors have made their books according to the prediloction or prejudice of each sect. Satisfied with a sonorous amen to accepted theology, they have often lost sight of poetical excellence; and a morbid feeling has been engendered which excluded the beautiful simply because it came from another sect than their own.

But these fallacies have wrought their own cure; and now, without relaxing their efforts to produce the new, Christian scholars are returning to the good old paths.

No one, to our knowledge, has yet attempted a great historic hymnal. This work remains to be done; but scholars of the present age have touched portions of the field. Among these are Caswell, a Roman Catholic clergyman, whose collection comprises the hymns of the Roman Breviary and those of the breviaries of Paris and Cluny, and also the hymns and sequences from the Missal. Dr. Neale, besides the Greek hymns mentioned, has also published mediæval Latin hymns; and many writers have given English renderings of special Greek and Latin hymns. Some of the favorites have been done into English very many times. It would be curious, for example, to collate the English versions of the *Dies Iræ*.

Although not directly a part of our subject, it may not be amiss here to set forth the true meaning and character of a hymn. In its technical Christian meaning, a hymn touches its Greek etymology: it is a poem in honor and praise of the Deity; not simply a *religious poem*, but, in general, an address of penitence or praise to the Almighty. We would not invariably insist upon the form of apostrophe; for, to borrow the idea of the British Critic, humility often imitates the Seraphim, who veil their faces and cry *one to another*, "Holy, Holy, Holy!" but it must be conceived in the spirit of penitent adoration and direct ascription of praise. A doctrinal poem setting forth the formularies of the Church is not a hymn; nor is such an epic, miscalled eclogue, as Pope's sparkling paraphrase from Isaiah; nor is a homily in verse, nor a set of expository couplets. The poem of Montgomery beginning,—

"Prayer is the soul's sincere desire,"

although extremely well expressed, has no element of a hymn. Nothing can be finer than the verses of Cowper beginning,—

"God moves in a mysterious way;"

but, from first to last, it is a solemn lesson to man, and not a tribute of praise to God. In proportion as a religious poem embodies the direct idea of *worship* it approaches the technical model. Such, for example, are many of the psalms of David, still used by the Church catholic in what a modern writer calls a *second intention;* that is, with a Christian adaptation. In this view of worship they are antiphonally rendered by double choirs, to give effect to the responsive meaning of their versicles. Such, too, are most of the hymns collected in the various breviaries, now generally known in spirited translations; and such are many of those of the Eastern Church, to which we have already referred.

Deviating somewhat from the model which we have presented are the Latin and Greek hymns intended for acts of special worship on the various feast and fast days of the Church; which, besides the ascriptions of praise, indicate or explain the character of the holy-day which they are designed to commemorate.

Let us venture to add that a hymn should be simple in language as well as fervent in thought, and should avoid rhetorical brilliancy and the art of the schools. It is designed for the great heart of Christendom, and not for the cultivated and scholarly few. Thus it has happened that the best hymns have been produced by writers of mediocrity, and not by the world's great poets. Milton's magnificent "Ode to the Nativity" is miscalled a hymn; and, although the greatest of English poets, he has produced no hymn which is a universal favorite; while many which are almost anonymous are very near the hearts of all Christian people.

It is a curious fact that, in the modern efforts to resuscitate, the true meaning of a hymn has been almost entirely lost sight of. We know of no collection, at least, in which it is the leading feature. To refer again to the hymns of Watts, we find a flood of religious poetry doing the office of exposition and exhortation, threatening, instructing, and alarming the sinner, encouraging the saint, describing the joys of heaven and the horrors of the second death, paraphrasing the inimitable Scriptures,—worthy, indeed, to be read and pondered, but certainly not designed to be sung by Christians who stand up, at the bidding of the minister, to "continue the worship of Almighty God." And yet in this indiscriminate manner have the books of psalms and hymns been collected in the churches. We do not include in this condemnation any collections but those designed for worship. The truly great work of Keble is a series of poems to illustrate and commemorate the holy-days of the Christian year. It was not designed for use in the churches; but each poem may be read with profit and pleasure as an exquisite sermon in verse, to supplement at home the church-services of the day. Were it not for their great length, however, they would be quite as appropriate as many of the hymns in our popular collections.

I have dwelt thus long upon the character of the hymn, to correct what I consider a prevailing error; but I would by no means exclude all the poems which do not come up to the rigorous standard proposed. Only let every one of them have an indirect bearing at least upon the topic of praise to God.

We must enter upon a new hymnic period; but it should not be characterized by frantic efforts to produce new hymns. We should seek to use the great wealth which is now our inheritance by carefully studying its treasures and by great sagacity in selecting from them. All new hymns should be subjected to rigorous criticism before being admitted to common use. Of one

5

thing we should be careful; and that is, in our first presentation
of an author not to tamper with his verse, but to leave it as he
wrote it. Such tampering is oftener done by sectarian prejudice
than by ignorance. Thus, the beautiful Litany Hymn of the
Episcopal Church, with the well-known refrain, "Hear our
solemn litany," was barbarously rendered, in one collection,
"Hear thy people when they cry." The meaning of this is
evident; but who can appreciate the ignorance of the collector
who rendered Cowper's beautiful lines, —

> "Deep in unfathomable mines
> Of never-failing skill,"

so as to make it read, "*with* never-failing skill," thus losing the
finest point of the imagery? It unfortunately happens, however,
that the alterations improperly made at first remain fixed, and
become so familiar in the ears of the people that a return to the
original is impossible. Such is the case in the hymn beginning,
"Rock of ages," the accepted version of which is greatly altered
from the original poem. I may seem to violate my own precept
with reference to this very hymn, as I have reproduced it from
the Episcopal Prayer-Book; but, if I have erred in so doing, it
will be easy for my readers, thus informed, to compare it with
the original.

As indicative of the prevailing spirit of the times, many
Christian bodies are engaged in preparing new collections of
psalms and hymns for public worship. The General Convention
of the Protestant Episcopal Church in 1862 appointed a com-
mittee on "Hymnody and Metrical Psalmody," to revise and
alter the psalms and hymns at the end of the Prayer-Book. The
committee consists of six bishops, five clergymen, and two lay-
men, and will make its report in 1865. They have before them
an important work; for the need of revision is great. The

psalms in metre are *paraphrases*, by no means so good as the prose version of the psalter, which might be appropriately chanted in their stead; and the collection of hymns is faulty, in my judgment, because many of them do not come up to the standard which I have presumed to lay down, and many others are far more valuable for their devout spirit than for poetical excellence. And yet it is true of both these classes that they have so identified themselves with the affections and devotions of Christian people in public worship, in private sorrows, and in holy joys, that to remove them would seem like cutting off a dear old friend on account of some personal deformity. It would be a thankless and disagreeable office to illustrate by special examples: any one that we might take would have many admirers among our readers, who would be pained by such an analysis.

But to return to this volume. A few beautiful pieces, old and new, have been brought together without any attempt at chronological arrangement, and yet, it is hoped, without a discordant note. It is but a reproduction of the old "Trisagion" melody, sung by many voices, ancient and modern, bursting loudly from the great heart of the Church to-day, and with chimings of mellower tones and still fainter utterance as we reach back to the apostolic times. Here are voices from all the centuries and from all branches of the Church. The "Kyrie and Christe Eleison" of the Greek Church chimes with the "Confiteor" and the "Agnus Dei" of the Latin Church of the Middle Ages; and both form a harmonious chord with the never-ending songs of the Anglican Church, and of those of millions of Christians of all denominations, who sound the praises or implore the atoning mercy of Him who is God of God, Light of Light, Very God of Very God,—the Lord Christ.

Most of the poems in this volume are hymns; but I have not

scrupled to introduce other religious poetry, to give a pleasant variety. The Greek hymns of Neale are most of them marked by their Greek captions: many of the Latin hymns will be recognized in a similar manner.

I desire to express my grateful acknowledgments to my friend the Rev. Dr. Washburn, late Rector of St. Mark's Church, Philadelphia, and now of Calvary, New York, for his admirable and scholarly translations of several beautiful Latin hymns; and I venture to express the hope that he will give to the world in book-form his researches and translations in that field. From other friends of taste I have received suggestions and assistance, and could have extended the volume greatly without exhausting the treasures at my disposal.

I cannot withhold my congratulations and thanks from the publishers for the magnificence of the art illustrations, for the beauty of the typography, and the splendid general appearance of this volume. The first impression is due to the publishers' merits; but I feel secure of that second and, I hope, more lasting one, which will be made upon all people of taste and piety by the perusal of many of these beautiful poems. If I am not mistaken, their devotion will be rekindled, and their taste gratified. They will experience a new pleasure in finding themselves brought into a new communion, bound by golden links to the saintly and loving hearts of those "holy men of old," of whom it may be said, with no irreverence, that, like the prophets, they spake as they were moved by the Holy Ghost.

HENRY COPPÉE.

THE PILGRIMS OF JESUS.

O HAPPY band of pilgrims,
　If onward ye will tread
With Jesus as your Fellow
　To Jesus as your Head!

6　　　　　　　　　　21

Oh, happy, if ye labor
  As Jesus did for men!
Oh, happy, if ye hunger
  As Jesus hungered then!

The Cross that Jesus carried
  He carried as your due:
The Crown that Jesus weareth
  He weareth it for you.

The Faith by which ye see Him,
  The Hope in which ye yearn,
The Love that through all troubles
  To Him alone will turn,—

What are they, but vaunt-couriers
  To lead you to His Sight?
What are they, save the effluence
  Of Uncreated Light?

The trials that beset you,
  The sorrows ye endure,
The manifold temptations
  That Death alone can cure,—

What are they, but His jewels
  Of right celestial worth?
What are they, but the ladder
  Set up to heaven on earth?

O happy band of pilgrims,
    Look upward to the skies.—
Where such a light affliction
    Shall win you such a prize!

St. Joseph of the Studium.

STARS OF THE MORNING.

Stars of the morning, so gloriously bright,
Filled with celestial resplendence and light;
These that, where night never followeth day,
Raise the Trishagion ever and aye:

These are Thy counsellors: these dost Thou own,
God of Sabaoth! the nearest Thy throne;
These are Thy ministers, these dost Thou send,
Help of the helpless ones! man to defend.

These keep the guard, amidst Salem's dear bowers:
Thrones, Principalities, Virtues, and Powers:
Where with the Living Ones, mystical Four,
Cherubim, Seraphim, bow and adore.

"Who like the Lord?" thunders Michael, the Chief:
Raphael, "the Cure of God," comforteth grief:
And, as at Nazareth, prophet of peace,
Gabriel, "the Light of God," bringeth release.

Then, when the earth was first poised in mid space,—
Then, when the planets first sped on their race,—
Then, when were ended the six days' employ,—
Then all the Sons of God shouted for joy.

Still let them succor us; still let them fight,
LORD of angelic hosts, battling for right!
Till, where their anthems they ceaselessly pour,
We with the Angels may bow and adore!

ST. JOSEPH OF THE STUDIUM.

❀

EVENING HYMN.

τὴν ἡμέραν διελθών.

THE day is past and over:
  All thanks, O Lord, to Thee!
I pray Thee that offenceless
  The hours of dark may be.
O Jesu! keep me in Thy sight
And save me through the coming night!

The joys of day are over:
  I lift my heart to Thee,
And call on Thee, that sinless
  The hours of sin may be.

O Jesu! make their darkness light,
And save me through the coming night!

The toils of day are over:
  I raise the hymn to Thee,
And ask that free from peril
  The hours of fear may be.
O Jesu! keep me in Thy sight
And guard me through the coming night!

Lighten mine eyes, O Saviour,
  Or sleep in death shall I;

7

And he, my wakeful tempter,
　　Triumphantly shall cry,
" He could not make their darkness light,
Nor guard them through the hours of night!"

Be Thou my soul's preserver,
　　O God! for Thou dost know
How many are the perils
　　Through which I have to go:
Lover of men, oh, hear my call,
And guard and save me from them all!

　　　　　　　　ST. ANATOLIUS.

———

"GOD OF GOD, LIGHT OF LIGHT, VERY GOD OF VERY GOD."

ζοφεράς τρικυμίας.

FIERCE was the wild billow;
　　Dark was the night;
Oars labored heavily;
　　Foam glimmered white;
Trembled the mariners;
　　Peril was high:
Then said the God of God,
　　—"Peace! It is I!"

Ridge of the mountain-wave,
  Lower thy crest!
Wail of Euroclydon,
  Be thou at rest!
Sorrow can never be,—
  Darkness must fly,—
Where saith the Light of Light,
  —" Peace! It is I!"

Jesu, Deliverer!
  Come Thou to me:
Soothe Thou my voyaging
  Over Life's sea!
Thou, when the storm of Death
  Roars, sweeping by,
Whisper, O Truth of Truth!
  —" Peace! It is I!"

ST. ANATOLIUS.

CHRISTMAS-TIDE.

μέγα καὶ παράδοξον θαῦμα.

A GREAT and mighty wonder!
  A full and holy cure!
The Virgin bears the Infant
  With Virgin-honor pure!

The Word is made Incarnate,
  And yet remains on high:
And Cherubim sing anthems
  To shepherds from the sky.

And we with them triumphant
  Repeat the hymn again:
" To God on high be glory,
  And peace on earth to men!"

While thus they sing your Monarch,
  Those bright Angelic bands,
Rejoice, ye vales and mountains!
  Ye oceans, clap your hands!

Since all He comes to ransom,
  By all be He adored,
The Infant born in Bethlehem,
  The Saviour and the Lord!

And idol forms shall perish,
And error shall decay,
And Christ shall wield His sceptre,
Our Lord and God for aye.

St. Anatolius.

ST. STEPHEN'S DAY.

τῷ Βασιλεῖ καὶ Δεσπότη.

THE Lord and King of all things
    But yesterday was born :
And Stephen's glorious offering
    His birthtide shall adorn.
No pearls of orient splendor,
    No jewels, can he show ;
But with his own true heart's blood
    His shining vestments glow.

Come, ye that love the Martyrs,
    And pluck the flowers of song,
And weave them in a garland
    For this our suppliant throng :
And cry, O thou that shinest
    In grace's brightest ray,
Christ's valiant Protomartyr,
    For peace and favor pray !

Thou first of all Confessors,
    Of all the Deacons crown,
Of every following athlete
    The glory and renown :

Make supplication, standing
  Before Christ's Royal Throne,
That He would give the Kingdom,
  And for our sins atone!

[With the above stanzas the reader may not be displeased to compare the celebrated sequence of Adam of St. Victor, *Heri mundus exultavit*, which has never yet, we believe, appeared in English.]

Heri mundus exultavit.

Yesterday with exultation
Joined the world in celebration
  Of her promised Saviour's birth :
Yesterday the Angel nation
Poured the strain of jubilation
  O'er the Monarch born on earth.

But to-day, o'er death victorious,
By his faith and actions glorious,
  By his miracles renowned,
Dared the Deacon Protomartyr
Earthly life for Heaven to barter,
  Faithful midst the faithless found.

Forward, champion, in thy quarrel!
Certain of a certain laurel,
  Holy Stephen, persevere!
Perjured witnesses confounding,
Satan's Synagogue astounding
  By thy doctrine true and clear.

Lo! in Heaven *thy* Witness liveth;
Bright and faithful proof He giveth
 Of His Martyr's full success:
Thou by name *a Crown* impliest;
Meetly then in pangs thou diest
 For the Crown of Righteousness!

For a crown that fadeth never,
Bear the torturer's brief endeavor;
 Victory waits to end the strife:
Death shall be thy birth's beginning,
And life's losing be the winning
 Of a true and better life.

Whom the Holy Ghost endueth,
Whom celestial light imbueth,
 Stephen penetrates the skies:
There God's fullest glory viewing,
There his victor strength renewing,
 For his near reward he sighs.

See, as Jewish foes invade thee,
See, how Jesus *stands* to aid thee;
 Stands, to guard His champion's death!
Cry that opened Heaven is shown thee:
Cry that Jesus waits to own thee:
 Cry it with thy latest breath!

As the dying Martyr kneeleth,
For his murderers he appealeth,
And his prayer their pardon sealeth,
 For their madness grieving sore;

Then in Christ he sleepeth sweetly,
Who his pattern kept completely,
And with Christ he reigneth meetly,
Martyr first-fruits, evermore!

PALM SUNDAY.

Ἰησοῦς ὑπὲρ τοῦ κόσμου.

Jesus, hastening for the world to suffer.
    Enters in, Jerusalem, to thee:
With His Twelve He goeth forth to offer
    That free Sacrifice He came to be.

They that follow Him with true affection
    Stand prepared to suffer for His Name:
Be we ready, then, for man's rejection,
    For the mockery, the reproach, the shame.

Now, in sorrow, sorrow finds its healing:
    In the form wherein our father fell,
Christ appears, those quickening Wounds revealing,
    Which shall save from sin and death and hell.

Now, Judea, call thy Priesthood nigh thee!
    Now for Deicide prepare thy hands!
Lo! thy Monarch, meek and gentle, by thee!
    Lo! the Lamb and Shepherd in thee stands!
9

To thy Monarch, Salem, give glad greeting!
Willingly he hastens to be slain,

For the multitude His entrance meeting
With their false Hosanna's ceaseless strain.
Blest is He that comes, they cry.
On the Cross for man to die!'

ST. ANDREW OF CRETE.

WHENCE SHALL MY TEARS BEGIN?

Πόθεν ἄρξομαι θρηνεῖν;

WHENCE shall my tears begin?
What first-fruits shall I bear
Of earnest sorrow for my sin?
Or how my woes declare?
O Thou, the Merciful and Gracious One!
Forgive the foul transgressions I have done.

With Adam I have vied,
Yea, passed him, in my fall;
And I am naked now, by pride
And lust made bare of all;
Of Thee, O God, and that Celestial Band,
And all the glory of the Promised Land.

No earthly Eve beguiled
My body into sin:
A spiritual temptress smiled,
Concupiscence within:
Unbridled passion grasp'd the unhallow'd sweet:
Most bitter—ever bitter—was the meat.

If Adam's righteous doom,
Because he dared transgress

Thy one decree, lost Eden's bloom
    And Eden's loveliness,
What recompense, O Lord, must I expect,
Who all my life Thy quickening laws neglect?

    By mine own act, like Cain,
      A murderer was I made:
    By mine own act my soul was slain,
      When Thou wast disobeyed:
And lusts each day are quickened, warring still
Against the soul with many a deed of ill.

    Thou formedst me of clay,
      O Heavenly Potter! Thou
    In fleshly vesture didst array,
      With life and breath endow.
Thou Who didst make, didst ransom, and dost know,
To Thy repentant creature pity show!

    My guilt for vengeance cries;
      But yet Thou pardonest all,
    And whom Thou lovest Thou dost chastise.
      And mourn'st for them that fall:
Thou, as a Father, mark'st our tears and pain,
And welcomest the prodigal again.

    I lie before Thy door,
      Oh, turn me not away!
    Nor in mine old age give me o'er
      To Satan for a prey!
But ere the end of life and term of grace,
Thou Merciful, my many sins efface!

The Priest beheld, and passed
The way he had to go :
A careless glance the Levite cast,
And left me to my woe :
But Thou, O Jesu, Mary's Son, console.
Draw nigh and succor me, and make me whole !

Thou Spotless Lamb divine,
Who takest sins away,
Remove far off the load that mine
Upon my conscience lay :
And, of thy tender mercy, grant Thou me
To find remission of iniquity !

ST. ANDREW OF CRETE.

--

THE GREAT FAST.

οὐ γὰρ βλέπεις τοὺς ταράττοντας.

CHRISTIAN, dost thou *see* them
On the holy ground,
How the troops of Midian
Prowl and prowl around?
Christian, up and smite them,
Counting gain but loss :
Smite them by the merit
Of the Holy Cross !

Christian, dost thou *feel* them,
How they work within,
Striving, tempting, luring,
Goading into sin?

Christian, never tremble!
Never be downcast!
Smite them by the virtue
Of the Lenten Fast!

Christian, dost thou *hear* them,
  How they speak thee fair?
"Always fast and vigil?
  Always watch and prayer?"
Christian, answer boldly :
  "While I breathe I pray :"
Peace shall follow battle,
  Night shall end in day.

"Well I know thy trouble,
  O My servant true ;
Thou art very weary,—
  I was weary too :
But that toil shall make thee,
  Some day, all Mine own :
But the end of sorrow
  Shall be near My Throne."

St. Andrew of Crete.

CHRISTOS ANESTI.

ἀναστάσεως ἡμέρα.

'Tis the Day of Resurrection :
  Earth, tell it out abroad!
The Passover of Gladness!
  The Passover of God!

From Death to Life Eternal,—
From Earth unto the sky,
Our Christ hath brought us over,
With hymns of victory.

Our hearts be pure from evil,
That we may see aright

The Lord in rays eternal
Of Resurrection-Light:
And, listening to His accents,
May hear, so calm and plain,
His own *All Hail!* and, hearing,
May raise the victor strain!

Now let the Heavens be joyful!
Let earth her song begin!
Let the round world keep triumph,
And all that is therein:
Invisible and visible,
Their notes let all things blend:
For Christ the Lord hath risen,—
Our Joy that hath no end.

ST. JOHN DAMASCENE.

STAND ON THY WATCH-TOWER.

ἐπὶ τῆς θείας φυλακῆς.

STAND on thy watch-tower, Habakkuk the Seer,
And show the Angel, radiant in his light:
To-day, saith he, Salvation shall appear,
Because the Lord hath risen, as God of might.

The male that opes the Virgin's womb is He;
The Lamb of Whom His faithful people eat:
Our truer Passover from blemish free;
Our very God, Whose Name is all complete.

11

Our cleansing Pascha, beauteous from his rest,
Behold the Sun of Righteousness arise.

Before the ark, a type to pass away,
    David of old time danced: we, holier race,
Seeing the Antitype come forth to-day,
    Hail with a shout Christ's own Almighty grace.

ST. JOHN DAMASCENE.

— —

LET US RISE IN EARLY MORNING.

ὀρθρίσωμεν ὄρθου βαθέυς.

LET us rise in early morning
    And, instead of ointments, bring
Hymns of praises to our Master,
    And his Resurrection sing:
We shall see the Sun of Justice
    Risen with healing on His wing.

Thy unbounded loving-kindness,
    They that groaned in Hades' chain,
Prisoners, from afar beholding,
    Hasten to the light again;
And to that eternal Pascha
    Wove the dance and raised the strain.

Go ye forth, His Saints, to meet Him!
    Go with lamps in every hand!

From the sepulchre He riseth:
  Ready for the Bridegroom stand:
And the Pascha of salvation
  Hail, with his triumphant band.

St. John Damascene.

THE FURNACE.

'Ο παῖδας ἐκ καμίνου.

WHO from the fiery furnace saved the Three,
  Suffers as mortal; that, His passion o'er,
This mortal, triumphing o'er death, might be
  Vested with immortality once more.
    He Whom our fathers still confessed
    God over all, forever blest.

The women with their ointment seek the tomb,
  And Whom they mourned as dead, with many a tear,
They worship now, joy dawning on their gloom,
  As Living God, as mystic Passover;
    Then to the Lord's Disciples gave
    The tidings of the vanquished grave.

We keep the festal of the death of death;
  Of hell o'erthrown; the first-fruits, pure and bright,

Of life eternal; and, with joyous breath,
   Praise Him that won the victory by His might,
      Him Whom our fathers still confessed
      God over all, forever blest.

All-hallowed festival, in splendor born!
   Night of salvation and of glory! Night
Foreheralding the Resurrection morn!
   When from the tomb the everlasting Light,
      A glorious frame once more his own,
      Upon the world in splendor shone.

                St. John Damascene.

JERUSALEM.

φωτίζου, φωτίζου.

Thou New Jerusalem, arise and shine!
   The glory of the Lord on thee hath risen
Sion, exult! rejoice with joy divine,
   Mother of God! Thy Son hath burst his prison.

O Heavenly Voice! O word of purest love!
   "Lo! I am with you alway to the end."
This is the anchor, steadfast from above,
   The golden anchor, whence our hopes depend.

            12

O Christ, our Pascha! greatest, holiest, best!
   God's Word and Wisdom and effectual Might!
Thy fuller, lovelier presence manifest
   In that eternal realm that knows no night!

St. John Damascene.

THE DAWN IS SPRINKLING.

Aurora jam spargit polum.

THE dawn is sprinkling in the east
Its golden shower, as day flows in;
Fast mount the pointed shafts of light;—
Farewell to darkness and to sin!

Away, ye midnight phantoms all!
Away, despondence and despair!
Whatever guilt the night has brought,
Now let it vanish into air.

So, Lord, when that last morning breaks
Which shrouds in darkness earth and skies,
May it on us, low bending here,
Arrayed in joyful light arise!

To God the Father glory be,
And to His sole-begotten Son;
The same, O Holy Ghost, to Thee,
While everlasting ages run.

FOR ALL SAINTS.

τὰς ἱδρὰς τὰς αἰωνίας.

THOSE eternal bowers
　Man hath never trod,
Those unfading flowers
　Round the Throne of God:
Who may hope to gain them
　After weary fight?
Who at length attain them
　Clad in robes of white?

He who gladly barters
　All on earthly ground;
He who, like the Martyrs,
　Says, "I WILL be crowned!"
He whose one oblation
　Is a life of love;
Clinging to the nation
　Of the Blest above.

Shame upon you, legions
　Of the Heavenly King,
Denizens of regions
　Past imagining!
13

What! with pipe and tabor
  Fool away the light,
When He bids you labor,—
  When He tells you,—" Fight!"

While I do my duty,
  Struggling through the tide,
Whisper Thou of beauty
  On the other side!
Tell who will the story
  Of our *now* distress:
Oh, the future glory!
  Oh, the loveliness!

St. John Damascene.

— - ———

FIX ME FIRMLY.

στερέωσόν με, Χριστέ.

"On the rock of Thy commandments
  Fix me firmly, lest I slide:
With the glory of Thy Presence
  Cover me on every side;
Seeing none save Thee is holy,
  God, forever glorified!"

New immortal out of mortal,
  New existence out of old :
This the Cross of Christ accomplished,
  This the Prophets had foretold :
So that we, thus newly quickened,
  Might attain the heavenly fold.

Thou who comprehendest all things,
  Comprehended by the tomb,
Gav'st Thy Body to the grave-clothes
  And the silence and the gloom ;
Till through fast-closed doors Thou camest
  Thy Disciples to illume.

Every nail-print, every buffet,
  Thou didst freely undergo,
As Thy Resurrection's witness
  To the Twelve Thou cam'st to show :
So that what *they* saw in vision,
  Future years by faith might know.

ST. JOHN DAMASCENE.

THE DARK MYSTERY.

μέγα τὸ μυστήριον.

"Christ, we turn our eyes to Thee,
And this mighty mystery!
Habakkuk exclaimed of old,
In the Holy Spirit bold,
'Thou shalt come in time appointed,
For the help of Thine anointed!'"

Taste of myrrh He deigned to know,
Who redeemed the source of woe:
Now He bids all sickness cease
Through the honey-comb of peace,
And to this world deigns to give
That sweet fruit by which we live.

Patient Lord! with loving eye
Thou invitest Thomas nigh;
Showing of that Wounded Side:
While the world is certified,
How the third day, from the grave,
Jesus Christ arose to save.

Blest, O Didymus, the tongue
Where that first confession hung :
First the Saviour to proclaim,
First the Lord of Life to name :
Such the graces it supplied,—
That dear touch of Jesu's side !

St. John Damascene.

— · · · · · —————

GOD COMES.

'Ὁ Κύριος ἔρχεται.

God comes !—and who shall stand before His fear?
Who bide His Presence, when He draweth near?
    My soul, my soul, prepare
    To kneel before Him there !

Haste,—weep,—be reconciled to Him before
The fearful judgment knocketh at the door,
    Where, in the Judge's eyes,
    All bare and naked lies.

Have mercy, Lord, have mercy, Lord, I cry,
When with Thine angels Thou appear'st on high,
    And each a doom shall herit
    According to his merit.

14

How can I bear Thy fearful anger, Lord?
I, that so often have transgress'd Thy word?
      But put my sins away,
      And spare me in that day!

O miserable soul, return, lament,
Ere earthly converse end, and life be spent:

Ere, time for sorrow o'er,
The Bridegroom close the door!

Yea, I have sinned, as no man sinned beside.
With more than human guilt my soul is dyed:
     But spare and save me here,
     Before that day appear!

Three Persons in one Essence uncreate,
On Whom, both Three and One, our praises wait,
     Give everlasting light
     To them that sing Thy might!

St. Theodore of the Studium.

CHRISTMAS DAY.

Χριστὸς γεννᾶται· δοξάσατε.

CHRIST is born! Tell forth his fame!
Christ from Heaven! His love proclaim!
Christ on earth! Exalt his Name!
Sing to the Lord, O world, with exultation!
Break forth in glad thanksgiving, every nation!
     For He hath triumphed gloriously!

Man, in God's own Image made,
Man, by Satan's wiles betrayed,
Man, on whom corruption preyed,

Shut out from hope of life and of salvation,
To-day Christ maketh him a new creation,
   For He hath triumphed gloriously!

For the Maker, when His foe
Wrought the creature death and woe,
Bowed the Heavens, and came below,
And, in the Virgin's womb His dwelling making,
Became True Man, man's very nature taking;
   For He hath triumphed gloriously!

He, the Wisdom, Word, and Might,
God, and Son, and Light of light,
Undiscovered by the sight
Of earthly monarch, or infernal spirit,
Incarnate was, that we might Heaven inherit;
   For He hath triumphed gloriously!

                  ST. COSMAS.

THE EXPRESS IMAGE.

τῷ πρὸ τῶν αἰώνων.

HIM, of the Father's very Essence
Begotten, ere the world began,
And, in the latter time, of Mary,
   Without a human sire, made Man:

Unto Him, this glorious morn,
Be the strain outpoured;
Thou that liftest up our horn,
Holy art thou, Lord!

The earthly Adam, erewhile quickened
By the blest breath of God on high,
Now made the victim of corruption,
By woman's guile betrayed to die,
He, deceived by woman's part,
Supplication poured;
Thou Who in my nature art,
Holy art Thou, Lord!

Thou, Jesus Christ, wast consubstantial
With this our perishable clay,
And, by assuming earthly nature,
Exaltedst it to heavenly day.
Thou That wast as mortal born,
Being God adored.
Thou That liftest up our horn,
Holy art Thou, Lord!

Rejoice, O Bethlehem, the city
Whence Judah's monarchs had their birth;
Where He that sitteth on the Cherubs,
The King of Israel, came on earth:
Manifested this blest morn,
As of old time never,
He hath lifted up our horn,
He shall reign forever!

ST. COSMAS.

16

THE GOD-MAN.

'Pά,βδος ἐκ τῆς ῥίζης.

Rod of the Root of Jesse,
  Thou, Flower of Mary born,
From that thick shady mountain
  Cam'st glorious forth this morn:
Of her, the Ever Virgin,
  Incarnate wast Thou made,
The immaterial Essence,
  The God by all obeyed!
      Glory, Lord, Thy servants pay
      To thy wondrous might to-day!

The Gentiles' expectation,
  Whom Jacob's words foretell,
Who Syria's pride shalt vanquish,
  Samaria's power shalt quell;
Thou from the Root of Judah
  Like some fair plant dost spring,
To turn old Gentile error
  To Thee, its God and King!
      Glory, Lord, Thy servants pay
      To Thy wondrous might to-day!

In Balaam's ancient vision
  The Eastern seers were skilled;
They marked the constellations,
  And joy their spirits filled:
For Thou, bright Star of Jacob,
  Arising in Thy might,
Didst call these Gentile first-fruits
  To worship in Thy light.
      They, in holy reverence bent,
      Gifts acceptable present.

As on a fleece descending
  The gentle dews distil,
As drops the earth that water,
  The Virgin didst Thou fill.
For Media, leagued with Sheba,
  Falls down and worships Thee:
Tarshish and Ethiopia,
  The Isles and Araby.
      Glory, Lord, Thy servants pay
      To Thy wondrous might to-day!

ST. COSMAS.

ART THOU WEARY?

κόπον τε καὶ κάματον.

ART thou weary, art thou languid.
   Art thou sore distrest?
"Come to Me,"—saith One,—"and, coming,
    Be at rest!"

Hath He marks to lead me to Him,
   If He be my Guide?
"In His Feet and Hands are Wound-prints,
     And His Side."

Is there Diadem, as Monarch,
   That His Brow adorns?
"Yea, a Crown, in very surety,—
     But of Thorns!"

If I find Him, if I follow,
   What His guerdon here?
"Many a sorrow, many a labor,
     Many a tear."

If I still hold closely to Him,
   What hath He at last?
"Sorrow vanquished, labor ended,
     Jordan past!"

If I ask Him to receive me,
   Will He say me nay?
"Not till earth, and not till heaven
     Pass away!"

Finding, following, keeping, struggling,
   Is He sure to bless?
"Angels, Martyrs, Prophets, Virgins,
     Answer, Yes!"

             St. Stephen the Sabaite.
16

GOD BLESSED FOREVER.

οἱ παῖδες εὐσεβείᾳ.

THE Holy Children boldly stand
Against the tyrant's dread command:
The kindled furnace they defy,—
No doom can shake their constancy:
They in the midmost flame confessed,
"God of our Fathers! Thou art blessed!"

The Shepherds keep their flocks by night;
The Heaven glows out with wondrous light;
The glory of the Lord is there,
The Angel-bands their King declare:
The watchers of the night confessed,
"God of our Fathers! Thou art blessed!"

The Angel ceased; and suddenly
Seraphic legions filled the sky:
Glory to God, they cry again:
Peace upon earth, good will to men:
Christ comes!—And they that heard confessed,
"God of our Fathers! Thou art blessed!"

What said the Shepherds? "Let us turn
This new-born miracle to learn."
To Bethlehem's gate their footsteps drew:
The Mother with the Child they view:
They knelt, and worshipped, and confessed,
"God of our Fathers! Thou art blessed!"

St. Cosmas.

OH, WONDROUS MYSTERY.

μυστήριον ξένον.

Oh, wondrous mystery, full of passing grace!
    The grot becometh Heaven: the Virgin's breast
The bright Cherubic Throne: the stall that place
    Where He, Who fills all space, vouchsafes to rest:
        Christ our God, to Whom we raise
        Hymns of thankfulness and praise.

The course propitious of the unknown Star
    The Magi followed on its heavenly way,
Until it led them, beckoning from afar,
    To where the Christ, the King of all things, lay:
        Him in Bethlehem they find,
        Born the Saviour of mankind.

"Where is the Child," they ask,—"the new-born King,
    Whose herald-light is glittering in the sky,—

To Whom our offerings and our praise we bring?"
And Herod's heart is troubled utterly.
Armed for war with God, in vain
Would he see that Infant slain.

ST. COSMAS.

— — - —

THAT FEARFUL DAY.

τὴν ἡμέραν τὴν φρικτήν.

THAT fearful day, that day of speechless dread,
When Thou shalt come to judge the quick and dead——
I shudder to foresee,
O God! what then shall be!

When Thou shalt come, angelic legions round,
With thousand thousands, and with trumpet sound;
Christ grant me in the air
With saints to meet Thee there!

Weep, O my soul, ere that great hour and day,
When God shall shine in manifest array,
Thy sin, that thou mayst be
In that strict judgment free!

The terror!—hell-fire fierce and unsufficed:
The bitter worm: the gnashing teeth:—O Christ,
Forgive, remit, protect;
And set me with the elect!

That I may hear the blessed voice that calls
The righteous to the joy of heavenly halls,
        And, King of Heaven, may reach
        The realm that passeth speech!

Enter Thou not in judgment with each deed,
Nor each intent and thought in strictness read;
        Forgive, and save me then,
        O Thou that lovest men!

Thee, One in Three blest Persons! Lord o'er all!
Essence of essence, Power of power, we call!
        Save us, O Father, Son,
        And Spirit, ever one!

                        ST. THEODORE OF THE STUDIUM.

17

ADAM'S COMPLAINT.

"THE Lord my Maker, forming me of clay,
By His own Breath the breath of life conveyed:
O'er all the bright new world He gave me sway,—
A little lower than the Angels made.
But Satan, using for his guile
The crafty serpent's cruel wile,
Deceived me by the Tree;
And severed me from God and grace,
And wrought me death, and all my race,
As long as time shall be.
O Lover of the sons of men!
Forgive, and call me back again!

"In that same hour I lost the glorious stole
Of innocence, that God's own Hands had made;
And now, the tempter poisoning all my soul,
I sit in fig-leaves and in skins arrayed:
I sit condemned, distressed, forsaken;
Must till the ground whence I was taken
By labour's daily sweat.
But Thou, that shalt hereafter come,
The offspring of a Virgin womb,
Have pity on me yet!
O turn on me those gracious eyes,
And call me back to Paradise!

"O glorious Paradise! O lovely clime!
O God-built mansions! Joy of every Saint!
Happy remembrance to all coming time!
Whisper, with all thy leaves, in cadence faint,
One prayer to Him Who made them all,
One prayer for Adam in his fall!—
That He, Who formed thy gates of yore,
Would bid those gates unfold once more
That I had closed by sin:
And let me taste that holy Tree
That giveth immortality
To them that dwell therein!
Or have I fallen so far from grace
That mercy hath for me no place?"

Adam sat right against the Eastern gate,
By many a storm of sad remembrance tost:
"Oh, me! so ruined by the serpent's hate!
Oh me! so glorious once, and now so lost!
So mad that bitter lot to choose!
Beguiled of all I had to lose!
Must I, then, gladness of my eyes,—
Must I, then, leave thee, Paradise,
And as an exile go?
And must I never cease to grieve
How once my God, at cool of eve,
Came down to walk below?
O Merciful! on Thee I call
O Pitiful! forgive my fall!"

St. Theophanes.

TRANSFIGURATION.

χορὸς 'Ισραήλ.

THE choirs of ransomed Israel,
  The Red Sea's passage o'er,
Upraised the hymn of triumph
  Upon the farther shore,
And shouted, as the foeman
  Was whelmed beneath the sea.
"Sing we to Judah's Saviour,
  For glorified is He!"

Amongst His Twelve Apostles
  Christ spake the Words of Life,
And showed a realm of beauty
  Beyond a world of strife:
"When all my Father's glory
  Shall shine expressed in Me,
Then praise Him, then exalt Him,
  For magnified is He!"

Upon the Mount of Tabor
  The promise was made good;
When, baring all the Godhead,
  In light itself He stood:

And they, in awe beholding,
　　The Apostolic Three,
Sang out to God their Saviour,
　　For magnified was He!

In days of old, on Sinai,
　　The Lord of Sabaoth came,
In majesty of terror,
　　In thunder-cloud and flame:
On Tabor, with the glory
　　Of sunniest light for vest,
The excellence of beauty
　　In Jesus was expressed.

All hours and days inclined there,
　　And did Thee worship meet;
The sun himself adored Thee,
　　And bowed him at Thy feet:
While Moses and Elias
　　Upon the Holy Mount
The coeternal glory
　　Of Christ our God recount.

Oh, holy, wondrous Vision!
　　But what, when, this life past,
The beauty of Mount Tabor
　　Shall end in Heaven at last?
But what, when all the glory
　　Of uncreated light
Shall be the promised guerdon
　　Of them that win the fight?

　　　　　　　St. Cosmas.

O FAITHFUL CROSS!

O FAITHFUL CROSS! O noblest tree!
In all our woods there's none like thee:
No earthly groves, no shady bowers,
Produce such leaves, such fruit, such flowers.
Sweet are the nails, and sweet the wood,
That bears a weight so sweet, so good.

Sing, O my tongue, devoutly sing
The glorious laurels of our King:
Sing the triumphant victory
Gained on the cross erected high;
Where man's Redeemer yields his breath,
And, dying, conquers hell and death.

With pity our Creator saw
His noblest work transgress his law,
When our first parents rashly ate
The fatal tree's forbidden meat;
He then resolved the cross's wood
Should make that tree's sad damage good.

By this wise method God designed
From sin and death to save mankind;

Superior art with love combines,
And arts of Satan countermines,
And where the traitor gave the wound,
There healing remedies are found.

When the full time decreed above
Was come to show this work of love,
Th' Eternal Father sends his Son,
The world's Creator, from his throne!
Who on our earth, this vale of tears,
Clothed with a virgin's flesh appears.

Thus God, made man, an infant lies,
And in the manger weeping cries:
His sacred limbs, by Mary bound,
The poorest tattered rags surround:
And God's incarnate feet and hands
Are closely bound with swathing bands.

Full thirty years were fully spent
In this our mortal banishment:
And then the Son of Man, decreed
For the lost sons of men to bleed,
And on the cross a victim laid,
The solemn expiation made.

Gall was his drink; his flesh they tear
With thorns and nails; a cruel spear
Pierces his side, from whence a flood
Streams forth, of water mixed with blood

With what a tide are washed again
The sinful earth, the stars, the main!

Bend, towering tree, thy branches bend,
Thy native stubbornness suspend :
Let not stiff nature use its force ;
To weaker saps have now recourse :
With softest arms receive thy load,
And gently bear our dying God.

On thee alone the Lamb was slain
That reconciled the world again ;
And when on raging seas was lost
The shipwrecked world and mankind lost,
Besprinkled with his sacred gore,
Thou safely brought them to the shore.

All glory to the sacred Three,
One undivided Deity :
To Father, Holy Ghost, and Son,
Be equal praise and homage done :
Let the whole universe proclaim
Of One and Three the glorious Name.

BURIAL OF THE DEAD.

Day of Wrath! Oh, day of mourning!
See fulfilled the prophets' warning!
Heaven and earth in ashes burning!
Oh, what fear man's bosom rendeth,
When from heaven the Judge descendeth,
On Whose sentence all dependeth!

Wondrous sound the trumpet flingeth,
Through earth's sepulchres it ringeth,
All before the Throne it bringeth;
Death is struck, and nature quaking,
All creation is awaking,
To its Judge an answer making.

Lo, the Book, exactly worded,
Wherein all hath been recorded!
Thence shall judgment be awarded.
When the Judge His seat attaineth,
And each hidden deed arraigneth,
Nothing unavenged remaineth.

What shall I, frail man, be pleading,
Who for me be interceding,
When the just are mercy needing?
King of Majesty tremendous,
Who dost free salvation send us,
Fount of pity, then befriend us!

Think, good Jesu, my salvation
Caused Thy wondrous Incarnation;
Leave me not to reprobation.

Faint and weary Thou hast sought me,
On the Cross of suffering bought me:
Shall such grace be vainly brought me?

Righteous Judge! for sin's pollution
Grant Thy gift of absolution
Ere that day of retribution.
Guilty, now I pour my moaning,
All my shame with anguish owning;
Spare, O God, Thy suppliant groaning.

Thou the sinful woman savedst;
Thou the dying thief forgavest;
And to me a hope vouchsafest.
Worthless are my prayers and sighing:
Yet, good Lord, in grace complying,
Rescue me from fires undying.

With thy favored sheep, oh, place me,
Nor among the goats abase me;
But to Thy right hand upraise me.
While the wicked are confounded,
Doomed to flames of woe unbounded,
Call me, with Thy saints surrounded.

Low I kneel, with heart-submission;
See like ashes my contrition;
Help me in my lost condition.

Ah! that day of tears and mourning!
From the dust of earth returning,
Man for judgment must prepare him;
Spare, O God, in mercy, spare him!
Lord all-pitying, Jesu blest,
Grant him Thine eternal rest.

DREAD FRAMER OF THE EARTH.

Æterne rerum conditor.

DREAD FRAMER of the earth and sky,
   Who dost the light and darkness give,
And all the cheerful change supply
   Of alternating morn and eve!

Light of the midnight traveller!
   Who dost divide the day from night!—
Loud crows the dawn's shrill harbinger,
   And wakens up the sunbeams bright.

Forthwith at this the darkness chill
   Retreats before the star of morn;
And from their busy schemes of ill
   The vagrant crews of night return.

Fresh hope at this the sailor cheers:
   The waves their stormy strife allay;
The Church's Rock at this, in tears,
   Hastens to wash his guilt away.

Arise ye, then, with one accord!
   Nor longer wrapt in slumber lie:

The cock rebukes all who their Lord
By sloth neglect, by sin deny.

At his clear cry joy springs afresh;
  Health courses through the sick man's veins;
The dagger glides into its sheath;
  The fallen soul her faith regains.

Jesu, look on us when we fall :—
　One momentary glance of Thine
Can from her guilt the soul recall
　To tears of penitence divine.

Awake us from false sleep profound,
　And through our senses pour Thy light;
Be Thy blest Name the first we sound
　At early dawn, the last at night.

To God the Father glory be,
　And to His sole-begotten Son;
The same, O Holy Ghost, to Thee,
　While everlasting ages run.

CASWALL.

SUNDAY.

Primo die quo Trinitas.

THIS day the blessed Trinity
　The universe began;
This day the world's Creator rose,
　O'ercoming death for man.

Casting betimes dull sloth away,
　We too will rise by night,
And, with the Prophet, seek the Lord
　Before the dawning light.

So may He stretch His hand to save,
    And hear us in His love,
And, cleansed from guilt, our souls restore
    To their blest home above.

So, while on this His holy Day,
    At this most sacred hour,

Our psalms amid the stillness rise,
  May He His blessings shower.

Father of lights! keep us this day
  From sinful passions free;
Grant us, in every word, and deed,
  And thought, to honor Thee.

Thou Lord of chastity divine!
  . Grant us the grace to quell
Those flames impure which, cherished here,
  Increase the flames of hell.

Saviour, of Thy sweet clemency
  Wash Thou our sins away;
Grant us Thy peace,—grant us with Thee
  The joys of endless day.

Father of mercies, hear our cry;
  Hear us, coequal Son,
Who reignest with the Holy Ghost,
  While ceaseless ages run.

CASWALL.

THE PASSION.

Mœrentes oculi spargite lachrymas.

Now let us sit and weep,
And fill our hearts with woe;
Pondering the shame and torments deep
Which God from wicked men did undergo.

See how the multitude,
With swords and staves, draw nigh;
See how they smite, with buffets rude,
That Head divine of awful majesty:

How, bound with cruel cord,
Christ to the scourge is given;
And ruffians lift their hands, unawed,
Against the King of kings and Lord of Heaven!

Hear it, ye people, hear!
Our good and gracious God,
Silent beneath the lash severe,
Stands with His sacred shoulders drenched in blood.

Oh, scene for tears! but now
The sinful race contrive
A torment new: deep in His brow,
With all their force, the jagged thorns they drive.

Then, roughly dragged to death,
Christ on the Cross is slain.
And, as He dies, with parting breath,
Into His Father's hands gives back His soul again.

To Him who so much bore
To gain for sinners grace,
Be praise and glory evermore
From the whole universal human race.

CASWALL.

O BLEST CREATOR.

Rerum Creator optime.

O BLEST Creator of the world,
    Look in Thy pity down;
Nor let the guilty sleep of sin
    Our souls in torpor drown.

Lord of all holiness, may we
    Find mercy in Thy sight!
Who, to set forth Thy glory, rise
    Before the morning light.

Who, as the holy Psalmist bids,
    Our hands thus early raise;
And in the midnight sing with Paul
    And Silas hymns of praise.

Jesu, to Thee our deeds we show,
    To Thee our hearts lie bare;

Oh, hearken to the sighs we pour,
　And in Thy mercy spare!

Father of mercies, hear our cry:
　Hear us, coequal Son,
Who reignest with the Holy Ghost
　While ceaseless ages run.

CASWALL.

NOW WITH THE RISING GOLDEN DAWN.

Lux ecce surgit aurea.

Now with the rising golden dawn,
　Let us, the children of the day,
Cast off the darkness which so long
　Has led our guilty souls astray.

Oh, may the morn, so pure, so clear,
　Its own sweet calm in us instil!—
A guileless mind, a heart sincere,
　Simplicity of word and will:

And ever, as the day glides by,
　May we the busy senses rein;
Keep guard upon the hand and eye,
　Nor let the body suffer stain!

For, all day long, on Heaven's high tower
　　There stands a Sentinel, who spies
Our every action, hour by hour.
　　From early dawn till daylight dies.

To God the Father glory be,
　　And to His sole-begotten Son ;
The same, O Holy Ghost, to Thee,
　　While everlasting ages run.

CASWALL.

HIS SACRED FEET.

Maria castis osculis.

His sacred feet with tears of agony
　　She bathes ; and prostrate on the earth adores ;
Steeps them in kisses chaste, and wipes them dry
With her own hair ; then forth her precious ointment pours.

Praise in the highest to the Father be ;
　　Praise to the mighty coeternal Son ;
　　And praise, O Spirit Paraclete, to Thee,
While ages upon everlasting ages run.

CASWALL.

HYMN FOR CONFIRMATION.

My God, accept my heart this day,
   And make it always Thine,—
That I from Thee no more may stray,
   No more from Thee decline.

Before the cross of Him who died,
   Behold, I prostrate fall:
Let every sin be crucified,—
   Let Christ be all in all!

Anoint me with Thy heavenly grace,
   Adopt me for Thine own,—
That I may see Thy glorious face
   And worship at Thy throne!

May the dear blood, once shed for me,
   My blest atonement prove,—
That I from first to last may be
   The purchase of Thy love!

Let every thought, and work, and word,
   To Thee be ever given:
Then life shall be Thy service, Lord.
   And death the gate of heaven!

BRYDGES.

SUNDAY MORNING.

Ad templa nos rursus vocat.

AGAIN the Sunday morn
  Calls us to prayer and praise,
Waking our hearts to gratitude
  With its enlivening rays.

But Christ yet brighter shone,
Quenching the morning beam,
When triumphing from death He rose,
And raised us up with Him.

When first the world sprang forth,
In majesty arrayed,
And bathed in streams of purest light,
What power was there displayed!

But, oh, what love! when Christ,
For our transgressions slain,
Was by th' Eternal Father raised
For us to life again!

His new-created world
The mighty Maker viewed,
With thousand lovely tints adorned,
And straight pronounced it good.

But, oh, much more He joyed
That selfsame world to see
Washed in the Lamb's all-saving Blood
From its impurity.

Nature each day renews
Her beauty evermore;
Whence to God's hidden Majesty
The soul is taught to soar.

But Christ, the Light of all,
  The Father's Image blest,
Gives us to see our God Himself
  In Flesh made manifest.

Blest Trinity, vouchsafe
  That, to thy guidance true,
What Thou forbiddest we may shun;
  What Thou commandest, do.

CASWALL.

THE ASCENSION.

WHY is thy face so lit with smiles,
  Mother of Jesus, why?
And wherefore is thy beaming look
  So fixed upon the sky?

From out thine overflowing eyes
  Bright lights of gladness part,
As though some gushing fount of joy
  Had broken in thy heart.

Mother, how canst thou smile to-day?
  How can thine eyes be bright,
When He, thy Life, thy Love, thine All,
  Hath vanished from thy sight?

His rising form on Olivet
  A summer's shadow cast;
The branches of the hoary trees
  Drooped as the shadow passed.

And as He rose, with all his train
  Of righteous souls around,
His blessing fell into thine heart,
  Like dew into the ground.

Down stooped a silver cloud from heaven,
  The Eternal Spirit's car.
And on the lessening vision went,
  Like some receding star.

The silver cloud hath sailed away,
  The skies are blue and free;
The road that vision took is now
  Sunshine and vacancy.

The Feet which Thou hast kissed so oft,
  Those living Feet, are gone;
Mother, thou canst but stoop and kiss
  Their print upon the stone.

He loved the Flesh thou gavest Him,
  Because it was from thee;
He loved it, for it gave Him power
  To bleed and die for me.

That flesh with its five witness Wounds
　　Unto His throne He bore,
For God to love, and spirits blest
　　To worship evermore.

Yes! He hath left thee, Mother dear:
　　His throne is far above;
How canst thou be so full of joy
　　When thou hast lost thy Love?

Oh, surely earth's poor sunshine now
　　To thee mere gloom appears,
When He is gone who was its Light
　　For Three-and-Thirty Years.

Why do not thy sweet hands detain
　　His Feet upon their way?
Oh, why doth not the Mother speak
　　And bid her Son to stay?

Ah, no! thy love is rightful love.
　　From all self-seeking free;
The change that is such gain to Him
　　Can be no loss to thee.

'Tis sweet to feel our Saviour's love,
　　To feel His presence near
Yet loyal love His glory holds
　　A thousand times more dear.

Who would have known the way to love
   Our Jesus as we ought,
If thou in varied joy and woe
   Hadst not that lesson taught?

Ah! never is our love so pure
   As when refined by pain,
Or when God's glory upon earth
   Finds in our loss its gain!

FABER.

MARY MAGDALEN.

To the hall of that feast came the sinful and fair;
She heard in the city that Jesus was there;
She marked not the splendor that blazed on their board;
But silently knelt at the feet of her Lord.

The hair from her forehead, so sad and so meek,
Hung dark o'er the blushes that burned on her cheek:
And so still and so lowly she bent in her shame,
It seemed as her spirit had flown from its frame.

The frown and the murmur went round through them all,
That one so unhallowed should tread in that hall;
And some said the poor would be objects more meet
For the wealth of the perfumes she showered at his feet.

24

She marked but her Saviour, she spoke but in sighs,
She dared not look up to the heaven of his eyes;
And the hot tears gushed forth at each heave of her breast,
As her lips to his sandals she throbbingly pressed.

On the cloud after tempests as shineth the bow,
In the glance of the sunbeam, as melteth the snow,
He looked on that lost one,—her sins were forgiven,
And Mary went forth in the beauty of heaven.

CALLANAN.

JERUSALEM THE GOLDEN.

JERUSALEM the golden,
  With milk and honey blest:
Beneath thy contemplation
  Sink heart and voice oppressed.

I know not, oh, I know not
  What joys await us there;
What radiancy of glory,
  What bliss beyond compare.

They stand, those halls of Sion,
  All jubilant with song,
And bright with many an angel,
  And all the martyr throng:

.The Prince is ever in them,
   The daylight is serene;
The pastures of the blessed
   Are decked in glorious sheen.

There is the throne of David;
   And there, from care released,
The shout of them that triumph.
   The song of them that feast:

And they, who with their Leader
   Have conquered in the fight,
Forever and forever
   Are clad in robes of white.

Oh, sweet and blessed country,
   The Home of God's elect!
Oh, sweet and blessed country,
   That eager hearts expect!

Jesu, in mercy bring us
   To that dear land of rest,
Who art, with God the Father.
   And Spirit, ever blest.

PRAYER OF THE CONTRITE SINNER.

Have mercy Thou, most gracious God,
    And my remittance sign;

The more Thy mercy shall accord,
　The greater glory Thine.

Thou surely hast not said in vain:
　" More joy in heaven is made
For the lost sheep that's found again,
　Than those which never strayed."

Helped by Thy grace, no more I'll stray,
　No more resist Thy voice;
Where Thou, good Shepherd, lead'st the way,
　That way shall be my choice.

Too long, alas! my wandering feet
　The crooked paths have trod;
Henceforth I'll follow, as is meet,
　The sure unerring road.

If casual falls retard my pace,
　With speed again I'll rise,
With speed I'll reassume my race,
　And run and gain the prize.

All praise, O Lord, to Thee alone,
　Below, as 'tis above:
And may Thy joys, Eternal One,
　Both draw and crown my love!

ROCK OF AGES.

Rock of Ages. cleft for me,
Let me hide myself in Thee :
Let the water and the blood.
From Thy wounded side which flowed.
Be of sin the double cure ;
Save from wrath and make me pure.

In my hand no price I bring,
Simply to Thy Cross I cling;
Naked. come to Thee for dress,
Helpless, look to Thee for grace.
Foul, I to the Fountain fly ;
Wash me, Saviour. or I die.

While I draw this fleeting breath,
When my eyes shall close in death,
When I rise to worlds unknown,
And behold Thee on Thy throne.
Rock of Ages, cleft for me.
Let me hide myself in Thee.

TOPLADY.

As many of our readers may not be familiar with Mr. Gladstone's Latin version of the hymn, " Rock of Ages, cleft for me," we subjoin it. It is given in a paper entitled " Mr. Gladstone as a Hymnologist :"—

JESUS, pro me perforatus,
Condar intra Tuum latus.
Tu per lympham profluentem.
Tu per sanguinem tepentem.
Impeccati mi redunda,
Tolle culpam. sordes munda.

Coram Te, nec justus forem
Quamvis tota vi laborem,
Nec si fide nunquam cesso,
Fletu stillans indefesso :
Tibi soli tantum munus :
Salva me, Salvator unus !

Nil in manu mecum fero,
Sed me versus Crucem gero ;
Vestimenta nudus oro,
Opem debilis imploro :
Fontem Christi quæro immundus.
Nisi laves, moribundus.

Dum hos artus vita regit ;
Quando nox sepulchro tegit ;
Mortuos cum stare jubes,
Sedens Judex inter nubes ;
Jesus. pro me perforatus,
Condar intra Tuum latus.

ST. FRANCIS XAVIER.

Lo! on the slope of yonder shore
    Beneath that lonely shed,
A saint hath found his conflicts o'er,
    And laid his dying head!

No gloom of fear hath glazed his eye,
    For, though loud billows roll,
The Aurora of Eternity
    Is dawning on his soul.

The glorious Saviour of his love
  Receives him in His arms,
And bears him, like a ransomed dove,
  Away from all alarms!

Champion of Jesus, man of God,
  Servant of Christ, well done!
Thy path of thorns hath now been trod,
  Thy red-cross crown is won!

O'er the wide waste of watery waves,
  And leagues on leagues of land,
Amidst a wilderness of graves,
  With death on every hand,

He flew to woo and win a world;
  That men might kiss the feet
Of Him whose banner he unfurled,—
  Father,—Son,—Paraclete.

His tongue, the Spirit's two-edged sword,
  Had magic in its blade;
For, while it smote with every word,
  It healed the wounds it made!

His lips were love, his touch was power,
  His thoughts were vivid flame,—
The flashes of a thunder-shower—
  Where'er, or when they came!
  26

Around him shone the light of life,
 Before him darkness fell :—
Satan receded from the strife,
 And sought his native hell!

Yet who so humbly walked as he,
 A conqueror in the field,
Wreathing the rose of victory
 Around his radiant shield?

As silvery clouds, at eventide,
 Float on the balmy gale,
Nor seem to heed the stars they hide
 Behind their fleecy veil,

So lowly sense of slightest worth
 Fresh graces o'er him threw;
For he unconscious lived on earth
 Of all the praise he drew!

Champion of Jesus, on that breast
 From whence thy fervor flowed,
Thou hast obtained eternal rest,
 The bosom of thy God!

BRYDGES.

IN MEMORIAM.

I saw two flowers at morning:
  The one was a full-blown rose:
And it lay at rest on a matron's breast.
  Like a gleam from the sunset close.
The other an opening rose-bud,
  As white as the sea-washed pearl;
And it graced, amid masses of dark-brown hair.
  The head of a beautiful girl.
And the flowers were types of these lovely ones,
  That mother and daughter fair,
Sending abroad, o'er life's arid road,
  Sweet perfume everywhere.

I saw two graves at even,
  Mid the fading light of day;
And there, at the head of the cherished dead,
  The morning flowerets lay.
And I cried, " O gentle flowers,
  Are those beautiful ones beneath?
Can aught so bright and so lovely
  Feel the withering grasp of Death?"
" Not so, not so," said the flowers;
  " 'Tis but dust beneath this sod;
For the holy souls on the sunset ray
  Went up to the bosom of God!"

H. COPPIE.

THE SINGERS.

God sent His Singers upon earth
With songs of sadness and of mirth,
That they might touch the hearts of men
And bring them back to heaven again.

The first, a youth, with soul of fire,
Held in his hand a golden lyre;

Through groves he wandered, and by streams,
Playing the music of our dreams.

The second, with a bearded face,
Stood singing in the market-place,
And stirred with accents deep and loud
The hearts of all the listening crowd.

A gray old man, the third and last,
Sang in cathedrals dim and vast,
While the majestic organ rolled
Contrition from its mouths of gold.

And those who heard the Singers three
Disputed which the best might be;
For still their music seemed to start
Discordant echoes in each heart.

But the great Master said, "I see
No best in kind, but in degree:
I gave a various gift to each,—
To charm, to strengthen, and to teach.

"These are the three great chords of might;
And he whose ear is tuned aright
Will hear no discord in the three,
But the most perfect harmony."

LONGFELLOW.

27

THE SLEEP.

"He giveth His beloved sleep."—Ps. cxxvii. 2.

Of all the thoughts of God that are
Borne inward unto souls afar
Along the Psalmist's music deep,
Now tell me if that any is,
For gift or grace, surpassing this:—
"He giveth His beloved sleep."

What would we give to our beloved?
The hero's heart, to be unmoved.
The poet's star-tuned harp, to sweep.
The patriot's voice, to teach and rouse,
The monarch's crown, to light the brows?—
"He giveth His beloved sleep."

What do we give to our beloved?
A little faith all undisproved,
A little dust to overweep,
And bitter memories to make
The whole earth blasted for our sake.
"He giveth His beloved sleep."

"Sleep soft, beloved!" we sometimes say,
But have no tune to charm away
Sad dreams that through the eyelids creep,
But never doleful dream again
Shall break the happy slumber, when
"He giveth His beloved sleep."

O earth, so full of dreary noises!
O men, with wailing in your voices!
O delvèd gold, the wailers heap!
O strife, O curse, that o'er it fall!
God strikes a silence through you all,
And "giveth His beloved sleep."

His dews drop mutely on the hill;
His cloud above it saileth still,

Though on its slope men sow and reap.
More softly than the dew is shed,
Or cloud is floated overhead,
"He giveth His beloved sleep."

Ay, men may wonder while they scan
A living, thinking, feeling man
Confirmed in such a rest to keep:
But angels say,—and through the word
I think their happy smile is *heard*,—
"He giveth His beloved sleep."

For me, my heart, that erst did go
Most like a tired child at a show,
That sees through tears the mummers leap,
Would now its wearied vision close,
Would childlike on His love repose
Who "giveth His beloved sleep."

And, friends, dear friends, when it shall be
That this low breath is gone from me,
And round my bier ye come to weep,
Let One, most loving of you all,
Say, "Not a tear must o'er her fall:
'He giveth His beloved sleep.'"

                              MRS. BROWNING.

THE SOUL-DIRGE.

THE organ played sweet music
  Whileas, on Easter-day,
All heartless from the altar
  The heedless went away;
And, down the broad aisle crowding,
  They seemed a funeral train,
That were burying their spirits
  To the music of that strain.

As I listened to the organ,
  And saw them crowd along,
I thought I heard two voices
  Speaking strangely, but not strong:
And one, it whispered sadly,
  Will ye also go away?
But the other spoke exulting,
  Ha! the soul-dirge,—hear it play!

Hear the soul-dirge! hear the soul-dirge!
  And see the feast divine!
Ha! the jewels of salvation,
  And the trampling feet of swine!
28

Hear the soul-dirge! hear the soul-dirge!
   Little think they, as they go,
What priceless pearls they tread on,
   Who spurn their Saviour so!

Hear the soul-dirge! hear the soul-dirge!
   It was dread to hear it play,
While the Famishing went crowding
   From the Bread of Life away:
They were bidden, they were bidden
   To their Father's festal board;
But they all, with gleeful faces,
   Turned their back upon the Lord.

You had thought the church a prison,
   Had you seen how they did pour
With giddy, giddy faces,
   From the consecrated door.
There was angels' food all ready,
   But the bidden—where were they?
O'er the highways and the hedges,
   Ere the soul-dirge ceased to play!

Oh, the soul-dirge, how it echoed
   The emptied aisles along,
As the open street grew crowded
   With the full outpouring throng!
And then—again the voices;
   Ha! the soul-dirge! hear it play!
And the pensive, pensive whisper,
   Will ye also go away?

Few, few were they that lingered
　To sup with Jesus there;
And yet, for all that spurned Him
　There was plenty, and to spare!
And now, the food of angels
　Uncovered to my sight,
All-glorious was the altar,
　And the chalice glittered bright.

Then came the hymn Trisagion,
　And rapt me up on high,
With angels and archangels
　To laud and magnify.
I seemed to feast in Heaven;
　And downward wafted then,
With angels chaunting round me,
　Good will and peace to men.

I may not tell the rapture
　Of a banquet so divine;
Ho! every one that thirsteth,
　Let him taste the bread and wine!
Hear the Bride and Spirit saying,
　Will ye also go away?
Or—go, poor soul, forever!
　Oh, the soul-dirge—hear it play!

　　　　　A. CLEVELAND COXE.

JAIRUS' DAUGHTER.

FRESHLY the cool breath of the coming eve
Stole through the lattice, and the dying girl

Felt it upon her forehead. She had lain
Since the hot noontide in a breathless trance,
Her thin, pale fingers clasped within the hand
Of the heart-broken Ruler, and her breast,
Like the dead marble, white and motionless.
The shadow of a leaf lay on her lips,
And, as it stirred with the awakening wind,
The dark lids lifted from her languid eyes,
And her slight fingers moved, and heavily
She turned upon her pillow. He was there,—
The same loved, tireless watcher, and she looked
Into his face until her sight grew dim
With the fast-falling tears, and, with a sigh
Of tremulous weakness, murmuring his name,
She gently drew his hands upon her lips,
And kissed it as she wept. The old man sunk
Upon his knees, and in the drapery
Of the rich curtains buried up his face;
And when the twilight fell, the silken folds
Stirred with his prayer; but the slight hand he held
Had ceased its pressure, and he could not hear,
In the dead, utter silence, that a breath
Came through her nostrils, and her temples gave
To his nice touch no pulse, and at her mouth
He held the lightest curl that on her neck
Lay with a mocking beauty, and his gaze
Ached with its deathly stillness.

                    It was night,
And softly o'er the Sea of Galilee
Danced the breeze-ridden ripples to the shore,

Tipped with the silver sparkles of the moon.
The breaking waves played low upon the beach
Their constant music, but the air beside
Was still as starlight, and the Saviour's voice,
In its rich cadences unearthly sweet,
Seemed like some just-born harmony in the air,
Waked by the power of wisdom. On a rock,
With the broad moonlight falling on His brow,
He stood and taught the people. At His feet
Lay His small scrip, and pilgrim's scallop shell,
And staff; for they had waited by the sea
Till He came o'er from Gadarene, and prayed
For His wont teachings as He came to land.
His hair was parted meekly on His brow,
And the long curls from off His shoulders fell
As He leaned forward earnestly, and still
The same calm cadence, passionless and deep,
And in His looks the same mild majesty,
And in His mien the sadness mixed with power,
Filled them with love and wonder.

                 Suddenly,
As on His words entrancedly they hung,
The crowd divided, and among them stood
Jairus the Ruler. With his flowing robe
Gathered in haste about his loins, he came,
And fixed his eyes on Jesus. Closer drew
The twelve disciples to their Master's side,
And silently the people shrunk away,
And left the haughty Ruler in the midst
Alone. A moment longer on the face

Of the meek Nazarene he kept his gaze,
And as the twelve looked on him. by the light
Of the clear moon, they saw a glistening tear
Steal to his silver beard, and, drawing nigh
Unto the Saviour's feet, he took the hem
Of His coarse mantle, and with trembling hands
Pressed it upon his lips, and murmured low,
"*Master, my daughter!*"

        The same silvery light
That shone upon the lone rock by the sea
Slept on the Ruler's lofty capitals
As at the door he stood, and welcomed in
Jesus and His disciples. All was still.
The echoing vestibule gave back the slide
Of their loose sandals, and the arrowy beam
Of moonlight, slanting to the marble floor,
Lay like a spell of silence in the rooms,
As Jairus led them on. With hushing steps
He trod the winding stair; but, ere he touched
The latchet, from within a whisper came:
"*Trouble the Master not,—for she is dead!*"
And his faint hand fell nerveless at his side,
And his steps faltered. and his broken voice
Choked in its utterance. But a gentle hand
Was laid upon his arm, and in his ear
The Saviour's voice sank thrillingly and low,
"*She is not dead, but sleepeth.*"

        They passed in.
The spice-lamps in the alabaster urns

Burned dimly, and the white and fragrant smoke
Curled indolently on the chamber walls.
The silken curtains slumbered in their folds,—
Not even a tassel stirring in the air,—
And as the Saviour stood beside the bed,
And prayed inaudibly, the Ruler heard
The quickening division of His breath
As He grew earnest inwardly. There came
A gradual brightness o'er His calm, sad face;
And, drawing nearer to the bed, He moved
The silken curtains silently apart
And looked upon the maiden.

              Like a form
Of matchless sculpture, in her sleep she lay,—
The linen vesture folded on her breast,
And over it her white, transparent hands,
The blood still rosy in their tapering nails.
A line of pearl ran through her parted lips,
And in her nostrils, spiritually thin,
The breathing curve was mockingly like life.
And round beneath the faintly-tinted skin
Ran the light branches of the azure veins;
And on her cheek the jet lash overlay,
Matching the arches pencilled on her brow.
Her hair had been unbound, and, falling loose
Upon her pillow, hid her small, round ears
In curls of glossy blackness, and about
Her polished neck, scarce touching it, they hung,
Like airy shadows floating as they slept.
'Twas heavenly beautiful. The Saviour raised

Her hand from off her bosom, and spread out
The snowy fingers in His palm, and said,
"*Maiden! Arise!*"—and suddenly a flush
Shot o'er her forehead, and along her lips
And through her cheek the rallied color ran,
And the still outline of her graceful form
Stirred in the linen vesture, and she clasped
The Saviour's hand, and, fixing her dark eyes
Full on His beaming countenance, AROSE.

N. P. WILLIS.

A HYMN FOR ALL NATIONS.

SUNG AT THE GREAT EXHIBITION IN LONDON, 1851,
AND TRANSLATED INTO THIRTY LANGUAGES
IN UPWARDS OF FIFTY VERSIONS.

GLORIOUS GOD, on Thee we call,
Father, Friend, and Judge of all;
Holy Saviour, heavenly King,
Homage to Thy throne we bring!

In the wonders all around
Ever is Thy Spirit found,
And of each good thing we see
All the good is born of Thee!

Thine the beauteous skill that lurks
Everywhere in Nature's works;
Thine is Art, with all its worth,
Thine each master-piece on earth.

Yea, and, foremost in the van,
Springs from Thee the Mind of Man;
On its light, for this is Thine,
Shed abroad the love divine!

Lo, our God, Thy children here
From all realms are gathered near,
Wisely gathered, gathering still,
For "peace on earth, towards men good will!"

May we, with fraternal mind,
Bless our Brothers of mankind!
May we, through redeeming love,
Be the blest of God above!

LITANY HYMN.

Saviour, when in dust to Thee
Low we bow th' adoring knee;
When, repentant, to the skies
Scarce we lift our streaming eyes;
Oh, by all Thy pains and woe,
Suffered once for man below,

Bending from Thy throne on high,
Hear our solemn litany.

By Thy birth and early years,
By Thy human griefs and fears,
By Thy fasting and distress
In the lonely wilderness:
By Thy victory in the hour
Of the subtle tempter's power;
Jesus, look with pitying eye;
Hear our solemn litany.

By Thine hour of dark despair,
By Thine agony of prayer,
By the purple robe of scorn,
By Thy wounds, Thy crown of thorn,
By Thy cross, Thy pangs and cries,
By Thy perfect sacrifice;
Jesus, look with pitying eye;
Hear our solemn litany.

By Thy deep expiring groan,
By the sealed sepulchral stone,
By Thy triumph o'er the grave,
By Thy power from death to save;
Mighty God, ascended Lord,
To Thy throne in heaven restored,
Prince and Saviour, hear our cry,
Hear our solemn litany.

GOD'S-ACRE.

I LIKE that ancient Saxon phrase, which calls
 The burial ground God's-Acre! It is just:
It consecrates each grave within its walls,
 And breathes a benison o'er the sleeping dust.

God's-Acre! Yes, that blessed name imparts
  Comfort to those who in the grave have sown
The seed that they had garnered in their hearts,—
  Their bread of life. alas! no more their own.

Into its furrows shall we all be cast,
  In the sure faith that we shall rise again
At the great harvest, when the archangel's blast
  Shall winnow, like a fan, the chaff and grain.

Then shall the good stand in immortal bloom
  In the fair gardens of that second birth,
And each bright blossom mingle its perfume
  With that of flowers which never bloomed on earth.

With thy rude ploughshare, Death, turn up the sod,
  And spread the furrow for the seed we sow;
This is the field and acre of our God,
  This is the place where human harvests grow!

LONGFELLOW.

--- —

CHRISTMAS EVEN.

Dark night broods o'er the city,
  Veiling the Temple's sheen,
And o'er the fields where shepherds keep
  Their sheep in Palestine.

31

Dark night is on the nations;
  Blind Pharisee and scribe
Grope vainly for the glory-light
  Of Judah's Lion tribe.

"Let there be light!" O Highest,
  As when this earth began;
The dawn shall rise on Nature,
  Bid Thy dawning rise on man!
The Temple hears no tidings,
  The Ark receives no light,
Not to Jerusalem the Fair
  Appear the Heralds bright.

Ah! not to Herod, Tetrarch,
  Nor to Sanhedrim old,
With pomp and ceremonial,
  Shall the glad news be told.
Though Anna dwelleth watching
  In chastity and tears,
Though Simeon to "depart in peace"
  Hath waited fourscore years;

Yet in the fields, to shepherds
  Like to the sheep they tend,
"The heavens declare the glory" forth,
  The highest heavens descend.
And now to you who, watching
  Like shepherds, seek the sign,
To you shall Christ the Lord be born
  As once in Palestine.

Fly open, hearts like mangers,
  For Him no fitting inn;
Prepare ye for the Infant God;
  Scourge out each brute-like sin;
Make ready gifts of innocence
  To greet the coming morn:
Then o'er your hearts His star shall rest,
  And there He shall be born.

                    H. Coppée.

THE ECHOES OF THE ANGELS' SONG.

"Glory be to God on high!"
  Such the wondrous story:
Hark! an earthly echo hears
  And sends back—the "Glory!"

"Peace on earth! good will to men!"
  Thus the song doth cease.
Stay: one strain of angel music
  Echoes back—the "Peace!"

                    H. Coppée.

THE FLOWERS OF GOD.

THE welcome flowers are blossoming,
    In joyous troops revealed;
They lift their dewy buds and bells
    In garden, mead, and field;
They lurk in every sunless path,
    Where forest children tread;

They dot, like stars, the sacred turf,
　Which lies above the dead.

They sport with every playful wind
　That stirs the blooming trees,
And laugh on every fragrant bush,
　All full of toiling bees:
From the green marge of lake and stream,
　Fresh vale and mountain sod,
They look in gentle glory forth,—
　The pure sweet flowers of God.

They come, with genial airs and skies,
　In summer's golden prime,
And to the stricken world give back
　Lost Eden's blissful clime:
Outshining Solomon they come,
　And go full soon away;
But yet, like him, they meekly breathe
　True wisdom while they stay.

" If God," they whisper, "smiles on us,
　And bids us bloom and shine,
Does He not mark, O faithless man!
　Each wish and want of thine?
Think, too, what joys await in Heaven
　The blest of human birth,
When rapture such as woos thee now
　Can reach the bad on earth!"

Redeemer of a fallen race,
  Most merciful of kings,
Thy hallowed words have clothed with power
  Those frail and beauteous things:
All taught by Thee, they yearly speak
  Their message of deep love,
Bidding us fix, for life and death,
  Our hearts and hopes above.

J. G. LYONS.

THE ROYAL BANNERS.

THE Royal Banners forward go;
The Cross shines forth in mystic glow;
Where He in flesh, our flesh Who made,
Our sentence bore, our ransom paid.

There whilst He hung, His sacred Side
By soldier's spear was opened wide,
To cleanse us in the precious flood
Of Water mingled with His Blood.

Fulfilled is now what David told
In true prophetic song of old,
How God the heathen's King should be;
For God is reigning from the tree.

O tree of glory, tree most fair,
Ordained those Holy Limbs to bear!
How bright in purple robe it stood,
The purple of a Saviour's Blood!

Upon its arms, like balance true,
He weighed the price for sinners due.—
The price which none but He could pay.—
And spoiled the spoiler of his prey.

To Thee, Eternal Three in One,
Let homage meet by all be done:
As by the Cross Thou dost restore,
So rule and guide us evermore.

O LIFE, O Death, O World, O Time,
  O Grave, where all things flow,
'Tis yours to make our lot sublime
  With your great weight of woe!

Though sharpest anguish hearts may wring,
  Though bosoms torn may be.
Yet suffering is a holy thing:
  Without it, what were we?

                    TRENCH.

The air is full of farewells to the dying,
  And mournings for the dead;
The heart of Rachel, for her children crying,
  Will not be comforted!

Let us be patient! These severe afflictions
  Not from the ground arise,
But oftentimes celestial benedictions
  Assume this dark disguise.

We see but dimly through the mists and vapors;
  Amid these earthly damps,
What seem to us but sad, funereal tapers
  May be heaven's distant lamps.

There is no Death! What seems so is transition.
  This life of mortal breath
Is but a suburb of the life elysian
  Whose portal we call Death.

She is not dead,—the child of our affection,—
  But gone unto that school
Where she no longer needs our poor protection,
  And Christ Himself doth rule.

In that great cloister's stillness and seclusion,
  By guardian angels led,
Safe from temptation, safe from sin's pollution,
  She lives, whom we call dead.

33

Day after day we think what she is doing
  In those bright realms of air;
Year after year, her tender steps pursuing,
  Behold her grown more fair.

Thus do we walk with her, and keep unbroken
  The bond which nature gives,
Thinking that our remembrance, though unspoken,
  May reach her where she lives.

Not as a child shall we again behold her;
  For when with raptures wild
In our embraces we again enfold her,
  She will not be a child;

But a fair maiden, in her Father's mansion,
  Clothed with celestial grace;
And beautiful with all the soul's expansion
  Shall we behold her face.

And though at times, impetuous with emotion
  And anguish long suppressed,
The swelling heart heaves moaning like the ocean,
  That cannot be at rest,—

We will be patient, and assuage the feeling
  We may not wholly stay;
By silence sanctifying, not concealing,
  The grief that must have way.

                              LONGFELLOW.

HAVE MERCY!

Lord, many times I am aweary quite
    Of mine own self, my sin, my vanity;
Yet be not Thou—or I am lost outright—
    Weary of. me.

And hate against myself I often bear,
    And enter with myself in fierce debate:
Take Thou my part against myself, nor share
    In that just hate!

Best friends might loathe us if what things perverse
    We know of our own selves they also knew:
Lord, Holy One, if Thou who knowest worse
    Shouldst loathe us too!

                    Trench.

JERUSALEM.

Jerusalem, thou City blest!
Dear vision of celestial rest,

Which far above the starry sky,
Piled up with living stones on high,
Art, as a Bride, encircled bright
With million angel forms of light:

Oh, wedded in a prosperous hour,
The Father's glory was thy dower;
The Spirit all His graces shed,
Thou peerless Queen, upon thy head:
When Christ espoused thee for His Bride,
O City bright and glorified!

Thy gates a pearly lustre pour;
Thy gates are open evermore;
And thither evermore draw nigh
All who for Christ have dared to die,
Or, smit with love of their dear Lord,
Have pains endured, and joys abhorred.

Thou too, O Church, which here we see!
No easy task hath builded thee.
Long did the chisels ring around;
Long did the mallets' blows rebound;
Long worked the head and toiled the hand,
Ere stood thy stones as now they stand!

BREVIARY.

THE GOD OF LOVE.

THE God of love my Shepherd is,
  And He that doth me feed;
While He is mine, and I am His,
  What can I want or need?

He leads me to the tender grass,
  Where I both feed and rest;
Then to the streams that gently pass:
  In both I have the best.

Or, if I stray, He doth convert,
  And bring my mind in frame.
And all this, not for my desert,
  But for His holy name.

Yea, in death's shady, black abode
  Well may I walk, nor fear:
For Thou art with me, and Thy rod
  To guide, Thy staff to bear.

Nay, Thou dost make me sit and dine,
  Ev'n in my enemies' sight.

My head with oil, my cup with wine
  Runs over, day and night.

Surely Thy sweet and wondrous love
  Shall measure all my days;
And, as it never shall remove,
  So neither shall my praise.

HERBERT.

STABAT MATER DOLOROSA.

At the cross her station keeping,
Stood the mournful mother weeping,
  Where He hung, the dying Lord:
For her soul, of joy bereavéd,
Bowed with anguish, deeply grievéd,
  Felt the sharp and piercing sword.

Oh, how sad and sore distresséd
Now was she, that mother blesséd
  Of the Sole-begotten One:
Deep the woe of her affliction
When she saw the Crucifixion
  Of her ever-glorious Son.

Who on Christ's dear mother gazing,
Pierced by anguish so amazing,
  Born of woman, would not weep?
Who on Christ's dear mother thinking,
Such a cup of sorrow drinking,
  Would not share her sorrows deep?

For His people's sins chastiséd,
She beheld her Son despiséd,
  Scourged, and crowned with thorns entwined,

Saw Him then from judgment taken,
And in death by all forsaken.
　　Till His spirit He resigned.

Jesu, may such deep devotion
Stir in me the same emotion,
　　Fount of love, Redeemer kind,
That my heart, fresh ardor gaining
And a purer love attaining,
　　May with Thee acceptance find!

A WREATH.

A WREATHÈD garland of deservèd praise,
Of praise deservèd, unto Thee I give;
I give to Thee, who knowest all my ways,
My crooked winding ways, wherein I live.
Wherein I die, not live; for life is straight,
Straight as a line, and ever tends to Thee,—
To Thee, who art more far above deceit
Than deceit seems above simplicity.
Give me simplicity, that I may live;
So live and like, that I may know Thy ways;
Know them and practise them. Then shall I give
For this poor wreath, give Thee a crown of praise.

HERBERT.

35

THE SILENT TOWER.

TINTADGEL bells ring o'er the tide !
The boy leans on his vessel side,—
He hears that sound, and dreams of home
Soothe the wild orphan of the foam.
    "Come to thy God in time !"
    Thus saith their pealing chime :
    "Youth, manhood, old age, past,
    Come to thy God at last !"

But why are Bottreaux' echoes still ?
Her tower stands proudly on the hill :
Yet the strange chough that home hath found,
The lamb lies sleeping on the ground.
    Come to thy God in time !
    Should be her answering chime,
    Come to thy God at last !
    Should echo on the blast.

The ship rode down with courses free,
The daughter of a distant sea ;
Her sheet was loose, her anchor stored, —
The merry Bottreaux bells on board.

The pilot heard his native bells
Hang on the breeze in fitful swells.

"Thank God!" with reverent brow, he cried,
"We make the shore with evening's tide!"
    Come to thy God in time!
    It was his marriage chime :—
    Youth, manhood, old age, past,
    His bell must ring at last!

Thank God, thou whining knave, on land!
But thank, at sea, the steersman's hand,
The captain's voice above the gale,—
Thank the good ship and ready sail!
    Come to thy God in time!
    Sad grew the boding chime :
    Come to thy God at last,—
    Boomed heavy on the blast!

Uprose that sea, as if it heard
The mighty Master's signal word!
What thrills the captain's whitening lip?
The death-groans of his sinking ship.
    Come to thy God in time!
    Swung deep the funeral chime :
    Grace, mercy, kindness, past.
    Come to thy God at last!

Long did the rescued pilot tell,
When gray hairs o'er his forehead fell,
While those around would hear and weep,
That fearful judgment of the deep!
    Come to thy God in time!
    He read his native chime :
    Youth, manhood, old age, past,
    His bell rung out at last!

Still, when the storm of Bottreaux' waves
Is wakening in his weedy caves,
Those bells that sullen surges hide
Peal their deep notes beneath the tide.
    Come to thy God in time!
    Thus saith the ocean chime:
    Storm, billow, whirlwind, past,
    Come to thy God at last.

R. S. HAWKER.

STRIVE.

STRIVE, when thou art called of God,
  When He draws thee by His grace,
Strive to cast away the load
  That would clog thee in the race!

Fight, though it may cost thy life,
  Storm the kingdom, but prevail;
Let not Satan's fiercest strife
  Make thee, warrior, faint or quail.

Wrestle, till through every vein
  Love and strength are glowing warm,—
Love that can the world disdain:
  Half-love will not bide the storm.

Wrestle, with strong prayers and cries,
  Think no time too much to spend,
Though the night be passed in sighs,
  Though all day thy voice ascend.

Hast thou won the pearl of price?
  Think not thou hast reached the goal,
Conquered every sin and vice
  That had power to harm thy soul.

Gaze with mingled joy and fear
  On the refuge thou hast found;
Know, while yet we linger here
  Perils ever hem us round.

Art thou faithful? then oppose
  Sin and wrong with all thy might;
Care not how the tempest blows,
  Only care to win the fight.

Art thou faithful? Wake and watch,
  Love with all thy heart Christ's ways,
Seek not transient ease to snatch,
  Look not for reward or praise.

Art thou faithful? Stand apart
  From all worldly hope and pleasure,
Yonder fix your hopes and heart,
  On the heaven where lies our treasure.

Soldiers of the Cross, be strong,
  Watch and war mid fear and pain,
Daily conquering woe and wrong,
  Till our King o'er earth shall reign!

WINKLER.

SUNDAY.

O DAY most calm, most bright!
The fruit of this, the next world's bud;
Th' indorsement of supreme delight,
Writ by a Friend, and with His blood;

The couch of time; care's balm and bay;—
The week were dark, but for thy light;
    Thy torch doth show the way.

    The other days and thou
Make up one man; whose face *thou* art.
Knocking at heaven with thy brow;
The worky days are the back-part;
The burden of the week lies there,
Making the whole to stoop and bow,
    Till thy release appear.

    Man had straight forward gone
To endless death. But thou dost pull
And turn us round, to look on one
Whom, if we were not very dull,
We could not choose but look on still;
Since there is no place so alone,
    The which He doth not fill.

    Sundays the pillars are
On which heaven's palace arched lies:
The other days fill up the spare
And hollow room with vanities.
They are the fruitful bed and borders
In God's rich garden; that is bare
    Which parts their ranks and orders.

    The Sundays of man's life,
Threaded together on Time's string,
37

Make bracelets to adorn the wife
Of the eternal, glorious King.
On Sunday, heaven's gate stands ope;
Blessings are plentiful and rife;
    More plentiful than hope.

    This day my Saviour rose,
And did inclose this light for His,
That, as each beast his manger knows,
Man might not of his fodder miss.
Christ hath took in this piece of ground,
And made a garden there, for those
    Who want herbs for their wound.

    The Rest of our creation
Our great Redeemer did remove
With the same shake which, at His passion,
Did th' earth, and all things with it, move.
As Samson bore the doors away,
Christ's hands, though nailed, wrought our salvation,
    And did unhinge that day.

    The brightness of that day
We sullied by our foul offence;
Wherefore that robe we cast away,
Having a new at His expense,
Whose drops of blood paid the full price
That was required to make us gay
    And fit for paradise.

    Thou art a day of mirth:
And, where the week-days trail on ground,

Thy flight is higher, as thy birth.
Oh, let me take thee at the bound.
Leaping with thee from seven to seven,
Till that we both, being tossed from earth,
    Fly hand in hand to heaven!

                  HERBERT.

AUDI, TELLUS, AUDI.

ADVENT HYMN OF THE ELEVENTH CENTURY.

HEAR, Earth, hear God's decree,
Cave of the mighty sea!
Hear, man! hear every one
Dwelling beneath the sun!

It cometh! it is near,
The day of wrath and fear!
Woe for that bitter day,
When shrinks the heaven away!
Gloweth the sun blood-red;
Afar the pale moon flieth;
Morning in blackness dieth:
Earthward the wan stars fall.
Upon that day of dread,
Woe! woe for sinners all!
In guilt and misery,
What shall our portion be?

                  WASHBURN.

THE CURATE.

NEAR yonder copse, where once the garden smiled,
And still where many a garden-flower grows wild.

There, where a few torn shrubs the place disclose.
The village preacher's modest mansion rose.
A man he was to all the country dear,
And passing rich with forty pounds a year;
Remote from towns he ran his godly race,
Nor e'er had changed, nor wished to change, his place;
Unskilful he to fawn, or seek for power,
By doctrines fashioned to the varying hour;
Far other aims his heart had learned to prize,
More bent to raise the wretched than to rise.
His house was known to all the vagrant train,
He chid their wanderings, but relieved their pain;
The long-remembered beggar was his guest,
Whose beard descending swept his aged breast;
The ruined spendthrift, now no longer proud,
Claimed kindred there, and had his claims allowed;
The broken soldier, kindly bade to stay,
Sate by his fire, and talked the night away;
Wept o'er his wounds, or, tales of sorrow done,
Shouldered his crutch, and showed how fields were won.
Pleased with his guests, the good man learned to glow,
And quite forgot their vices in their woe:
Careless their merits or their faults to scan,
His pity gave ere charity began.

Thus to relieve the wretched was his pride,
And e'en his failings leaned to virtue's side;
But in his duty prompt at every call,
He watched and wept, he prayed and felt for all;
And, as a bird each fond endearment tries
To tempt its new-fledged offspring to the skies,

33

He tried each art, reproved each dull delay,
Allured to brighter worlds, and led the way.

Beside the bed where parting life was laid,
And sorrow, guilt, and pain, by turns dismayed,
The reverend champion stood. At his control,
Despair and anguish fled the struggling soul;
Comfort came down the trembling wretch to raise,
And his last faltering accents whispered praise.

At church, with meek and unaffected grace,
His looks adorned the venerable place;
Truth from his lips prevailed with double sway,
And fools, who came to scoff, remained to pray.
The service past, around the pious man,
With ready zeal, each honest rustic ran;
E'en children followed, with endearing wile,
And plucked his gown, to share the good man's smile.
His ready smile a parent's warmth exprest,
Their welfare pleased him, and their cares distrest;
To them his heart, his love, his griefs, were given,
But all his serious thoughts had rest in heaven.
As some tall cliff that lifts its awful form,
Swells from the vale, and midway leaves the storm,
Though round its breast the rolling clouds are spread,
Eternal sunshine settles on its head.

GOLDSMITH.

CASTLES.

Let them that would build castles in the air
Vault thither, without step or stair,
Instead of feet to climb, take wings to fly,
And think their turret's top the sky.
But let me lay all my foundations deep,
And learn, before I run, to creep.
Who digs through rocks to lay his ground works low
May in good time build high, and sure, though slow.

CHRISTOPHER HARVEY.

GOD IN NATURE.

Go forth, my heart, and seek delight
In all the gifts of God's great might,
    These pleasant summer hours :
Look how the plains for thee and me
Have decked themselves most fair to see,
    All bright and sweet with flowers.

The trees stand thick and dark with leaves,
And earth o'er all her dust now weaves
    A robe of living green ;
Nor silks of Solomon compare
With glories that the tulips wear,
    Or lilies' spotless sheen.

The lark soars singing into space,
The dove forsakes her hiding-place,
    And coos the woods among ;
The richly-gifted nightingale
Pours forth her voice o'er hill and dale,
    And floods the fields with song.

Here with her brood the hen doth walk,
There builds and guards his nest the stork,
    The fleet-winged swallows pass ;

The swift stag leaves his rocky home,
And down the light deer bounding come
　　To taste the long rich grass,

The brooks rush gurgling through the sand,
And from the trees on either hand
　　Cool shadows o'er them fall;
20

The meadows at their side are glad
With herds; and, hark! the shepherd lad
    Sends forth his mirthful call.

And humming, hovering to and fro,
The never-wearied swarms forth go   ,
    To seek their honeyed food;
And through the vine's yet feeble shoots
Stream daily upwards from her roots
    New strength and juices good.

The corn springs up, a wealth untold,
A sight to gladden young and old,
    Who now their voices lift ·
To Him who gives such plenteous store,
And makes the cup of life run o'er
    With many a noble gift.

Thy mighty working, mighty God,
Wakes all my powers; I look abroad
    And can no longer rest:
I too must sing when all things sing,
And from my heart the praises ring
    The Highest loveth best.

I think, Art Thou so good to us,
And scatterest joy and beauty thus
    O'er this poor earth of ours;
What nobler glories shall be given
Hereafter in Thy shining heaven,
    Set round with golden towers!

What thrilling joy when on our sight
Christ's garden beams in cloudless light,
    Where all the air is sweet,
Still laden with the unwearied hymn
From all the thousand seraphim
    Who God's high praise repeat!

Oh, were I there! Oh that I now,
Dear God, before Thy throne could bow,
    And bear my heavenly palm!
Then like the angels would I raise
My voice, and sing Thy endless praise
    In many a sweet-toned psalm.

Nor can I now, O God, forbear,
Though still this mortal yoke I wear,
    To utter oft Thy name;
But still my heart is bent to speak
Thy praises; still, though poor and weak,
    Would I set forth Thy fame.

But help me; let Thy heavenly showers
Revive and bless my fainting powers,
    And let me thrive and grow
Beneath the summer of Thy grace,
And fruits of faith bud forth apace
    While yet I dwell below.

And set me, Lord, in Paradise
When I have bloomed beneath these skies
    Till my last leaf is flown;

Thus let me serve Thee here in time,
And after, in that happier clime,
   And Thee, my God. alone!

PAUL GERHARDT.

——

JAM MŒSTA QUIESCE QUERELA.

PRUDENTIUS. FIFTH CENTURY.

No more, ah, no more sad complaining,
   Resign these fond pledges to earth;
Stay, mothers, the thick-falling tear-drops:
   This death is a heavenly birth.

What mean these still caverns of marble,
   Fair shrines that the dear ashes keep?
How sweetly they tell of the loved ones,
   Not dead, but soft resting in sleep!

What though on the pale, icy forehead
   No gleam of the intellect break?
A moment it slumbers, till nobler
   Its powers in their beauty awake.

Soon, soon through the motionless body
   The warm, loving life-tide shall pour,
And, blushing with joy, shall revisit
   The home it has dwelt in before

These clods, 'neath the hillock reposing,
   Long wasting in silent decay,
Shall follow the souls that have loved them,
   On wingéd winds soaring away.

So green from the seed springs the blossom,
   Long perished, long hid in the mould;
And fresh from the turf, it remembers
   The wide-waving harvests of old.

Take, Earth, to thy bosom so tender,
   Take, nourish this body. How fair,
How noble in death! we surrender
   These relics of man to thy care.

This, this was the home of the spirit,
   Once built by the breath of our God;
And here, in the light of His wisdom,
   Christ, Head of the risen, abode.

Guard well the dear treasure we lend thee:
   The Maker, the Saviour of men
Shall never forget His belovéd,
   But claim His own likeness again.

Speed on, perfect year, to the morning;
   God's fulness shall dawn on the just,
And thou, open grave, shalt restore us
   This holy, unchangeable dust.

                WASHBURN.

THE CROSS.

Are thy toils and woes increasing?
Are the Foe's attacks unceasing?

Look with Faith unclouded,
Gaze with eyes unshrouded,
On the Cross!

Dost thou fear that strictest trial?
Tremblest thou at Christ's denial?
Never rest without it,
Clasp thine arms about it,—
That dear Cross!

Diabolic legions press thee?
Thoughts and works of sin distress thee?
It shall chase all terror,
It shall right all error,—
That sweet Cross!

Draw'st thou nigh to Jordan's river?
Shouldst thou tremble? Need'st thou quiver?
No, if by it lying,—
No, if on it dying,—
On the Cross!

Say, then, "Master, while I cherish
That sweet hope, I cannot perish!
After this life's story,
Give Thou me the glory
For the Cross!"

ST. METHODIUS.

GOD'S WORD.

On, blest were the accents of early creation,
    When the Word of Jehovah came down from above,
In the clods of the earth to infuse animation,
    And wake their cold atoms to life and to love!

And mighty the tones which the firmament rended,
   When on wheels of the thunder, and wings of the wind.
By lightning, and hail, and thick darkness attended,
   He uttered on Sinai His laws to mankind.

And sweet was the voice of the First-Born of Heaven
   (Though poor His apparel, though earthly His form),
Who said to the mourner, "Thy sins are forgiven!"
   "Be whole!" to the sick, and "Be still!" to the storm.

O Judge of the world, when, arrayed in Thy glory,
   Thy summons again shall be heard from on high,
While nature stands trembling and naked before Thee,
   And waits on Thy sentence to live or to die;

When the Heaven shall fly fast from the sound of Thy
     thunder,
   And the sun in Thy lightnings grow languid and pale,
And the sea yield her dead, and the Tomb cleave asunder,
   In the hour of Thy terrors, let mercy prevail!

                HEBER.

11

TO MONT BLANC.

Hast thou a charm to stay the morning star
In his steep course? So long he seems to pause
On thy bald awful head O sovereign Blanc!
The Arve and Arveiron at thy base
Rave ceaselessly; but thou, most awful Form,
Risest from forth thy silent sea of pines,
How silently! Around thee and above
Deep is the air and dark, substantial, black,

An ebon mass: methinks thou piercest it,
As with a wedge! But when I look again,
It is thine own calm home, thy crystal shrine,
Thy habitation from eternity!
O dread and silent Mount, I gazed upon thee
Till thou, still present to the bodily sense,
Didst vanish from my thought: entranced in prayer,
I worshipped the Invisible alone.

Yet, like some sweet beguiling melody,
So sweet we know not we are listening to it,
Thou, the mean while, wast blending with my thought,
Yea, with my life and life's own secret joy,
Till the dilating soul, enrapt, transfused,
Into the mighty vision passing—there
As in her natural form, swelled vast to Heaven!

Awake, my soul! not only passive praise
Thou owest! not alone these swelling tears,
Mute thanks, and secret ecstasy! Awake,
Voice of sweet song! Awake, my heart, awake!
Green vales and icy cliffs, all join my hymn.

Thou first and chief, sole sovereign of the Vale!
Oh, struggling with the darkness all the night,
And visited all night by troops of stars,
Or when they climb the sky or when they sink;
Companion of the morning star at dawn,
Thyself Earth's rosy star, and of the dawn
Coherald: wake, oh, wake, and utter praise!
Who sank thy sunless pillars deep in earth?

Who filled thy countenance with rosy light?
Who made thee parent of perpetual streams?

And you, ye five wild torrents fiercely glad!
Who called you forth from night and utter death.
From dark and icy caverns called you forth,
Down those precipitous, black, jagged rocks,
Forever shattered and the same forever?
Who gave you your invulnerable life,
Your strength, your speed, your fury, and your joy,
Unceasing thunder and eternal foam?
And who commanded (and the silence came),
Here let the billows stiffen and have rest?

Ye ice-falls! ye that from the mountain's brow
Adown enormous ravines slope amain—
Torrents, methinks, that heard a mighty voice,
And stopped at once amid their maddest plunge!
Motionless torrents, silent cataracts,
Who made you glorious as the gates of Heaven
Beneath the keen full moon? Who bade the sun
Clothe you with rainbows? Who, with living flowers
Of loveliest blue, spread garlands at your feet?—
God! let the torrents, like a shout of nations,
Answer! and let the ice-plains echo, God!
God! sing, ye meadow-streams, with gladsome voice!
Ye pine-groves, with your soft and soul-like sounds!
And they too have a voice, yon piles of snow,
And in their perilous fall shall thunder, God!

Ye living flowers that skirt the eternal frost!
Ye wild goats sporting round the eagle's nest!

Ye eagles, playmates of the mountain-storm!
Ye lightnings, the dread arrows of the clouds!
Ye signs and wonders of the element!
Utter forth God, and fill the hills with praise!

Thou too, hoar Mount, with thy sky-pointing peaks
Oft from whose feet the avalanche, unheard,
Shoots downward, glittering through the pure serene
Into the depth of clouds, that veil thy breast,—
Thou too again, stupendous Mountain, thou
That as I raise my head, a while bowed low
In adoration, upward from thy base
Slow travelling with dim eyes suffused with tears,
Solemnly seemest, like a vapory cloud,
To rise before me—Rise, oh, ever rise,
Rise like a cloud of incense, from the earth!
Thou kingly Spirit throned among the hills,
Thou dread ambassador from Earth to Heaven,
Great hierarch! tell thou the silent sky,
And tell the stars, and tell yon rising sun,
Earth, with her thousand voices, praises God.

COLERIDGE.

A MIDNIGHT HYMN.

WHERE'ER I am, whate'er I see,
Eternal Lord, is full of Thee!
I feel Thee in the gloom of night;
I see Thee in the morning light.

When care distracts my anxious soul,
Thy grace can every thought control;
Thy word can still the troubled heart,
And peace and confidence impart.

If pain invade my broken rest,
Or if corroding griefs molest,
Soon as the Comforter appears,
My sighs are hushed, and dried my tears.

Thy wisdom guides, Thy will directs,
Thy arm upholds, Thy power protects;
With Thee when I at dawn converse,
The shadows sink, the clouds disperse.

Then, as the sun illumes the skies,
Oh, Sun of Righteousness, arise!
Dispel the fogs of mental night,
Being of Beings, Light of Light.

HANNAH MORE.

Felicia Hemans

THE TRAVELLER'S EVENING SONG.

FATHER, guide me! Day declines,
Hollow winds are in the pines;
Darkly waves each giant bough
O'er the sky's last crimson glow;
Hushed is now the convent's bell,
Which erewhile with breezy swell

From the purple mountains bore
Greetings to the sunset-shore.
Now the sailor's vesper-hymn
　　　Dies away.
Father, in the forest dim,
　　　Be my Stay!

In the low and shivering thrill
Of the leaves that late hung still;
In the dull and muffled tone
Of the sea-wave's distant moan:
In the deep tints of the sky,
There are signs of tempest nigh.
Ominous, with sullen sound,
Falls the closing dusk around.
Father, through the storm and shade
　　　O'er the wild.
Oh, be Thou the lone one's Aid,—
　　　Save Thy child!

Many a swift and sounding plume
Homewards, through the boding gloom,
O'er my way hath flitted fast
Since the farewell sunbeam passed
From the chestnut's ruddy bark,
And the pools, now lone and dark,
Where the wakening night-winds sigh
Through the long reeds mournfully.
Homeward, homeward, all things haste.
　　　God of might,
Shield the homeless midst the waste.—
　　　Be his Light!

43

In his distant cradle-nest,
Now my babe is laid to rest;
Beautiful his slumber seems
With a glow of heavenly dreams.
Beautiful, o'er that bright sleep,
Hang soft eyes of fondness deep.
Where his mother bends to pray
For the loved and far-away.
Father, guard that household bower,
          Hear that prayer!
Back, through Thine all-guiding power,
          Lead me there!

Darker, wilder grows the night:
Not a star sends quivering light
Through the massy arch of shade
By the stern old forest made.
Thou to whose unslumbering eyes
All my pathway open lies,
By Thy Son, who knew distress
In the lonely wilderness,
Where no roof to that blest head
          Shelter gave,
Father, through the time of dread,
          Save, oh, save!

Mrs. Hemans.

THE ODOR.

How sweetly doth MY MASTER sound; MY MASTER!
  As ambergris leaves a rich scent
      Unto the taster:
  So do these words a sweet content,
An oriental fragrancy: MY MASTER!

With these all day I do perfume my mind,
  My mind even thrust into them both:
      That I might find
  What cordials make this curious broth,
This broth of smells, that feeds and fats my mind.

MY MASTER, shall I speak? Oh. that, to Thee,
  MY SERVANT were a little so.
      As flesh may be:
  That these two words might creep and grow
To some degree of spiciness to Thee!

Then should the Pomander, which was before
  A speaking sweet, mend by reflection,
    And tell me more.
  For pardon of my imperfection
Would warm and work it sweeter than before.

For when MY MASTER (which alone is sweet,
  And even in my unworthiness pleasing)
    Shall call, and meet
  My SERVANT, as Thee not displeasing;
That call is but the breathing of the sweet.

This breathing would with gains, by sweetening me
  (As sweet things traffic when they meet),
    Return to Thee;
  And so this new commerce and sweet
Should, all my life, employ and busy me.

HERBERT.

Gleams upon our dark path flinging,
    Cutting short each night begun;
Now Thy herald cock is singing
    To our chant, and calls the Sun.

And the morning star replies,
    And unlocks the imprisoned day,
And the ungodly bandit flies
    From his haunt and from his prey.

Shrill it sounds, the storm relenting
    Soothes the weary seaman's ears;
Once it wrought a great repenting,
    When the Church's rock shed tears.

Rouse we; let the blithesome cry
    Of that bird our hearts awaken,
Chide the slumberers as they lie,
    And convince the sin-o'ertaken.

Hope and health are in his strain
    To the fearful and the ailing;
Murder sheathes his blade profane,
    Faith revives where faith was failing.

Jesu, Master, when we sin,
    Turn on us Thy healing face;
It will melt the offence within
    Into penitential grace.

44

Beam on our bewildered mind,
Till its dreamy shadows flee;
Stones cry out where Thou hast shined,
Jesu, musical with Thee.

LOVE OF JESUS.

I LOVE Thee, O most gracious Lord,
Not that Thou sav'st me by Thy word;
Nor yet because Thy wrath shall doom
Those loving not to endless gloom.

Thou, Thou, my Jesus, full of grace,
Didst me upon the cross embrace;
Didst bear the nails, the bloody spear,
The great disgrace, the rabble's jeer.

Innumerable griefs were Thine,
Great sweats, and anguish, Lord of mine!
The pangs of death, and all for me,
That I, poor wretch, might come to Thee!

Then why not love with all my heart?
O Jesus, most beloved Thou art!
Not that Thou sav'st my soul above,
Nor me condemn'st, do Thee I love.

Not for the hope of sure reward,
But for Thy love, O blessed Lord!
My love is Thine, and e'er shall be,
Because, my King, Thou reign'st o'er me!

                        C. C. Cox.

THE TRAVELLER'S RETURN.

Joy! the lost one is restored!
Sunshine comes to hearth and board
From the far-off countries old
Of the diamond and red gold;
From the dusky archer bands,
Roamers of the fiery sands;
From the desert winds, whose breath
Smites with sudden silent death;
He hath reached his home again,
          Where we sing
In Thy praise a fervent strain,
          God our King!

Mightiest, unto Thee he turned
When the noonday fiercest burned;
When the fountain springs were far,
And the sounds of Arab war
Swelled upon the sultry blast,
And the sandy columns past,
Unto Thee he cried; and Thou,
Merciful, didst hear his vow!

Therefore, unto Thee again
     Joy shall sing
Many a sweet and thankful strain,
     God our King!

Thou wert with him on the main,
And the snowy mountain-chain,
And the rivers dark and wide,
Which through Indian forests glide.
Thou didst guard him from the wrath
Of the lion in his path,
And the arrows on the breeze,
And the drooping poison trees;
Therefore, from the household train
     Oft shall spring
Unto Thee a blessing strain,
     God our King!

Thou to his lone watching wife
Hast brought back the light of life;
Thou hast spared his loving child
Home to greet him from the wild.
Though the suns of eastern skies
On his cheek have set their dyes,
Though long toils and sleepless cares
On his brow have blanched the hairs,
Yet the night of fear is flown,
He is living, and our own!
Brethren, spread his festal board,
Hang his mantle on his sword,
With the armor on the wall,
While this long, long silent hall
15

Joyfully doth hear again
    Voice and string
Swell to Thee the exulting strain,
    God our King!

Mrs. Hemans.

DAILY BREAD.

Day by day the manna fell;
Oh to learn this lesson well!
Still by constant mercy fed,
Give us, Lord, our daily bread.

"Day by day" the promise reads;
Daily strength for daily needs:
Cast foreboding fears away;
Take the manna of to-day.

Lord, our times are in Thy hand:
All our sanguine hopes have planned
To Thy wisdom we resign,
And would mould our wills to Thine.

Thou our daily task shalt give;
Day by day to Thee we live;
So shall added years fulfil
Not our own, our Father's will.

Oh to live exempt from care
By the energy of prayer;
Strong in faith, with mind subdued,
Glowing yet with gratitude!

NOTHING FAIR ON EARTH I SEE.

Nothing fair on earth I see
But I straightway think on Thee;
Thou art fairest in my eyes,
Source in whom all beauty lies!

When I see the reddening dawn
And the golden sun of morn,
Quickly turns this heart of mine
To Thy glorious form divine.

Oft I think upon Thy light
When the gray morn breaks the night;
Think, what glories lie in Thee,
Light of all Eternity!

When I see the moon arise
'Mid Heaven's thousand golden eyes,
Then I think, more glorious far
Is the Maker of yon star.

Or I think in spring's sweet hours,
When the fields are gay with flowers,
As their varied hues I see,
What must their Creator be!

When along the brook I wander,
Or beside the fountain ponder,
Straight my thoughts take wing and mount
Up to Thee, the purest Fount.

Sweetly sings the nightingale;
Sweet the flute's soft plaintive tale;
Sweeter than their richest tone
Is the name of Mary's Son.

Sweetly all the air is stirred
When the Echo's call is heard;
But no sounds my heart rejoice
Like to my Beloved's voice.

Come, then, fairest Lord, appear,
Come, let me behold Thee here;
I would see Thee face to face,
On Thy proper light would gaze.

Take away these veils that blind,
Jesus, all my soul and mind;
Henceforth ever let my heart
See Thee truly as Thou art!

ANGELUS.

ONWARD.

Come, brethren, let us go!
The evening closeth round,
'Tis perilous to linger here
On this wild desert ground.
Take courage as ye wend
On towards eternity;
From strength to strength your course shall be,
And good at last your end.

We shall not rue our choice,
Though strait our path and steep;
We know that He who called us here
His word shall ever keep.
Then follow, trusting; come,
And let each set his face
Toward yonder fair and blessed place,
Intent to reach our home.

The body and the house
Deck not, but deck the heart
With all your powers; we are but guests,
Ere long we must depart.
Ease brings disease; content
Howe'er his lot may fall,
A pilgrim bears and bows to all,
For soon the time is spent.

Come, children, let us go!
Our Father is our guide;
And when the way grows steep and dark,
He journeys at our side.
Our spirits He would cheer;
The sunshine of His love
Revives and helps us as we rove:
Ah, blest our lot e'en here!

Each hasten bravely on;
Not yet our goal is near:
Look to the fiery pillar oft,
That tells the Lord is here.

Onward your glances send,
.. Love beckons us, nor think
That they who following chance to sink
Shall miss their journey's end.

Come, children, let us go!
We travel hand in hand;
Each in his brother finds his joy
In this wild stranger land.
As children let us be,
Nor by the way fall out;
The angels guard us round about,
And help us brotherly.

The strong be quick to raise
The weaker when they fall;
Let love and peace and patience bloom
In ready help for all.
In love yet closer bound,
Each would be least, yet still
On love's fair path most pure from ill,
Most loving, would be found.

Come, wander on with joy,
For shorter grows the way;
Each rising sun brings on the time
When in the grave we lay
The body down; a while
Have truth and courage yet,
Your hopes above more fully set,
Careless of things more vile.

It will not last for long;
A little farther roam;
It will not last much longer now
　Ere we shall reach our home;
　There shall we ever rest,
　　There with our Father dwell,
　　With all the saints who served Him well,
　There truly, deeply blest.

For this all things we dare,—
'Tis worth the risk, I trow,—
Renouncing all that clogs our course,
　Or weighs us down below.
　O world, thou art too small;
　　We seek another, higher,
　　Whither Christ guides us ever nigher,
　Where God is all in all.

Friend of our perfect choice,
Thou Joy of all that live,
Being that know'st not chance or change,
　What courage dost Thou give!
　All beauty, Lord, we see,
　　All bliss and life and love,
　　In Him in whom we live and move,
　And we are glad in Thee!

TERSTEEGEN.

GREAT FAITH.

I MARKED a rainbow in the north,
   What time the wild autumnal sun
From his dark veil at noon looked forth,
   As glorying in his course half done,
Flinging soft radiance far and wide
Over the dusky heaven and bleak hill-side.

It was a gleam to Memory dear;
   And as I walk and muse apart,

When all seems faithless round and drear,
   I would revive it in my heart,
And watch how light can find its way
To regions farthest from the fount of day.

Light flashes in the gloomiest sky,
   And Music in the dullest plain,
For there the lark is soaring high
   Over her flat and leafless reign,
And chanting in so blithe a tone,
It shames the weary heart to feel itself alone.

Brighter than rainbow in the north,
   More cheery than the matin lark,
Is the soft gleam of Christian worth
   Which on some holy house we mark;
Dear to the pastor's aching heart
To think, where'er he looks, such gleam may have a part;

May dwell, unseen by all but Heaven,
   Like diamond blazing in the mine;
For ever, where such grace is given,
   It fears in open day to shine,
Lest the deep stain it owns within
Break out, and Faith be shamed by the believer's sin.

In silence and afar they wait,
   To find a prayer their Lord may hear:
Voice of the poor and desolate,
   You best may bring it to His ear.
Your grateful intercessions rise
With more than royal pomp, and pierce the skies.

Happy the soul whose precious cause
    You in the Sovereign Presence plead :
"This is the lover of Thy laws,
    The friend of Thine in fear and need :"
For to the poor Thy mercy lends
That solemn style, "Thy nation and Thy friends."

He too is blest whose outward eye
    The graceful lines of art may trace,
While his free spirit, soaring high,
    Discerns the glorious from the base :
Till out of dust his magic raise
A home for prayer and love, and full harmonious praise,

Where, far away and high above,
    In maze on maze the trancéd sight
Strays, mindful of that heavenly love
    Which knows no end in depth or height,
While the strong breath of Music seems
To waft us ever on, soaring in blissful dreams.

What though in poor and humble guise
    Thou here didst sojourn, cottage-born ?
Yet from Thy glory in the skies
    Our earthly gold Thou dost not scorn.
For Love delights to bring her best,
And where Love is, that offering evermore is blest.

Love on a Saviour's dying head
    Her spikenard drops unblamed may pour,
May mount His cross, and wrap Him dead
    In spices from the golden shore :

Risen, may embalm His sacred name
With all a Painter's art, and all a Minstrel's flame.

Worthless and lost our offerings seem,
    Drops in the ocean of His praise:
But Mercy with her genial beam
    Is ripening them to pearly blaze.
To sparkle in His crown above,
Who welcomes here a child's as there an angel's love.

KEBLE.

CATECHISM.

OH, say not, dream not, heavenly notes
    To childish ears are vain,
That the young mind at random floats,
    And cannot reach the strain.

Dim or unheard, the words may fall,
    And yet the Heaven-taught mind
May learn the sacred air, and all
    The harmony unwind.

Was not our Lord a little child,
    Taught by degrees to pray,

48

By father dear and mother mild
Instructed day by day?

And loved He not of Heaven to talk
With children in His sight.

To meet them in His daily walk,
  And to His arms invite?

What though around His throne of fire
  The everlasting chant
Be wafted from the seraph choir
  In glory jubilant?

Yet stoops He, ever pleased to mark
  Our rude essays of love,
Faint as the pipe of wakening lark
  Heard by some twilight grove:

Yet is He near us, to survey
  These bright and ordered files,
Like spring-flowers in their best array,
  All silence and all smiles.

Save that each little voice in turn
  Some glorious truth proclaims,
What sages would have died to learn,
  Now taught by cottage dames.

And if some tones be false or low,
  What are all prayers beneath,
But cries of babes, that cannot know
  Half the deep thought they breathe?

In His own words we Christ adore,
  But angels, as we speak,

Higher above our meaning soar
    Than we o'er children weak;

And yet His words mean more than they,
    And yet He owns their praise:
Why should we think He turns away
    From infants' simple lays?

KEBLE.

MY FATHER'S AT THE HELM.

'Twas when the sea's tremendous roar
    A little bark assailed,
And pallid fear, with awful power,
    O'er each on board prevailed:

Save one, the captain's darling son,
    Who fearless viewed the storm,
And playful with composure smiled
    At danger's threatening form.

"Why sporting thus," a seaman cried,
    "Whilst sorrows overwhelm?"
"Why yield to grief?" the boy replied;
    "My father's at the helm."

Despairing soul, from thence be taught
　　How groundless is thy fear;
Think on what wonders Christ has wrought,
　　And He is always near.

Safe in His hands, whom seas obey,
　　When swelling billows rise,
Who turns the darkest night to day,
　　And brightens lowering skies:

Though thy corruptions rise abhorred,
　　And outward foes increase,
.'Tis but for Him to speak the word,
　　And all is hushed to peace.

Then upward look, howe'er distressed:
　　Jesus will guide thee home,
To that blest port of endless rest,
　　Where storms shall never come.

ABIDE WITH ME.

ABIDE with me. Fast falls the eventide;
The darkness thickens: Lord, with me abide;
When other helpers fail, and comforts flee,
Help of the helpless, oh, abide .with me!

Swift to its close ebbs out life's little day;
Earth's joys grow dim, its glories pass away;
Change and decay in all around I see;
O Thou who changest not, abide with me.

Not a brief glance I beg, a passing word,
But as Thou dwell'st with Thy disciples, Lord,—

Familiar, condescending, patient, free,
Come not to sojourn, but abide with me.

Come not in terrors, as the King of kings,
But kind and good, with healing in Thy wings;
Tears for all woes, a heart for every plea;
Come. Friend of sinners, thus abide with me!

Thou on my head in early youth didst smile,
And, though rebellious and perverse meanwhile,
Thou hast not left me, oft as I left Thee;
On to the close, O Lord, abide with me.

I need Thy presence every passing hour:
What but Thy grace can foil the tempter's power?
Who like Thyself my Guide and Stay can be?
Through cloud and sunshine, oh, abide with me!

I fear no foe, with Thee at hand to bless:
Ills have no weight, and tears no bitterness:
Where is Death's sting? where, Grave, thy victory?
I triumph still, if Thou abide with me!

Hold Thou Thy cross before my closing eyes,
Shine through the gloom, and point me to the skies:
Heaven's morning breaks, and earth's vain shadows flee:
In life, in death, O Lord, abide with me.

                                    LYTE.

CUR MUNDUS MILITAT?

Why battles all the world
For its vain glory,
Whose bravest happiness
Is transitory?

So soon its brittle power
  A light touch shaketh,
Even as a vase of clay
  In pieces breaketh.

Write words upon the ice,
  And trust their staying,
Sooner than idle cheats
  Of earth decaying.

Flattered with baubles gay,
  In Truth's mask hiding,
Thy life's a little day
  Of false confiding.

Better to plant thy trust
  In wise men's teaching,
Than for the wretched gauds
  Of Fortune reaching.

False are its very dreams,
  And false its pleasing,
Its labors and its lusts
  A hollow leasing.

Say, where is Solomon,
  Of wisdom vaunted,
Or stoutest Samson now,
  The chief undaunted?

Say, where is Absalom,
  Of beauty royal,

50

And Jonathan, the heart
　To friendship loyal?

Where hath the Cæsar left
　His empire splendid?
Where Dives' banqueting
　In sorrow ended?

Say, where is Tully's voice,
　In senates burning?
And the wise Stagyrite,
　Master of learning?

Such leaders of renown;
　Such bygone spaces;
Such stately brows of old,
　Such kingly races;

Such potentates of earth,
　The boast of story:—
One flashing of an eye,
　And gone their glory!

How brief a holyday
　Man's pomp abideth,
And all his pleasure gay
　A shadow glideth!

Feast·of the crawling worm!
　Dust to dust crumbled!
Drop of the morning dew!
　Be thy pride humbled.

Even to-morrow lies
  Veiled from thy blindness;
Crowd thou to-day with deeds
  Of loving-kindness.

This glory of the flesh,
  Which man paradeth,
The Holy Book doth call
  A flower that fadeth.

Even as the shrivelled leaf
  On the wind sweeping,
So drops the life of man,
  To darkness creeping.

Call not thine own whate'er
  A moment liveth;
The world shall snatch again
  All that it giveth.

Ponder the things above!
  There thy heart's treasure!
Happy, who knows to scorn
  The low world's pleasure!

WASHBURN.

BITTER REPENTANCE.

"And is there in God's world so drear a place
Where the loud bitter cry is raised in vain?

Where tears of penance come too late for grace,
　As on the uprooted flower the genial rain?

'Tis even so: the sovereign Lord of souls
　Stores in the dungeon of His boundless realm
Each bolt, that o'er the sinner vainly rolls,
　With gathered wrath the reprobate to whelm.

Will the storm hear the sailor's piteous cry,
　Taught to mistrust, too late, the tempting wave
When all around he sees but sea and sky,
　A God in anger, a self-chosen grave?

Or will the thorns that strew intemperance' bed
　Turn with a wish to down? will late remorse
Recall the shaft the murderer's hand has sped,
　Or from the guiltless bosom turn its course?

Then may the unbodied soul in safety fleet
　Through the dark curtains of the world above,
Fresh from the stain of crime, nor fear to meet
　The God whom here she would not learn to love:

Then is there hope for such as die unblest,
　That angel wings may waft them to the shore:
Nor need the unready virgin strike her breast,
　Nor wait desponding round the bridegroom's door.

But where is then the stay of contrite hearts?
　Of old they leaned on Thy eternal word,

But with the sinner's fear their hope departs,
   Fast linked as Thy great Name to Thee, O Lord.

That Name, by which Thy faithful oath is past,
   That we should endless be, for joy or woe :—
And if the treasures of Thy wrath could waste,
   Thy lovers must their promised Heaven forego.

But ask of elder days, earth's vernal hour,
   When in familiar talk God's voice was heard,
When at the Patriarch's call the fiery shower
   Propitious o'er the turf-built shrine appeared.

Watch by our father Isaac's pastoral door,—
   The birthright sold, the blessing lost and won,
Tell, Heaven has wrath that can relent no more,
   The Grave, dark deeds that cannot be undone.

We barter life for pottage ; sell true bliss
   For wealth or power, for pleasure or renown ;
Thus, Esau-like, our Father's blessing miss,
   Then wash with fruitless tears our faded crown.

Our faded crown, despised and flung aside,
   Shall on some brother's brow immortal bloom ;
No partial hand the blessing may misguide,
   No flattering fancy change our Monarch's doom:

His righteous doom, that meek true-hearted Love
   The everlasting birthright should receive,

The softest dews drop on her from above,
   The richest green her mountain garland weave :

Her brethren, mightiest, wisest, eldest-born,
   Bow to her sway, and move at her behest :
Isaac's fond blessing may not fall on scorn,
   Nor Balaam's curse on Love, which God hath blest.

                    KEBLE.

A TRUE HYMN.

   My Joy, my Life, my Crown !
   My heart was meaning all the day,
     Somewhat it fain would say ;
And still it runneth, muttering up and down,
With only this, My Joy, my Life, my Crown !

   Yet slight not these few words ;
    If truly said, they may take part
     Among the best in art.
The fineness, which a hymn or psalm affords,
Is, when the soul unto the lines accords.

   He, who craves all the mind,
   And all the soul, and strength, and time.
    If the words only rhyme,

Justly complains that somewhat is behind
To make his verse, or write a hymn in kind.

Whereas, if the heart be moved,
Although the verse be somewhat scant,
  God doth supply the want.
As when the heart says, sighing to be approved,
"Oh, could I love!" and stops: God writeth, Loved.

HERBERT.

—

LOVE OF GOD.

I LOVE Thee, O Thou God of mine,
  Because Thou first hast lovéd me:
And all my liberty resign
  That I may willing follow Thee.

Nothing that memory can suggest,
  But doth with Thy effulgence blend;
The mind's extremest range, at best,
  Thy greatness fails to comprehend.

Nothing, O Lord, will I desire
  Not sanctioned by Thy holy will;
All things are Thine that I acquire,
  All I bestow, Thy bounty still.

Take from me all Thy gifts reveal;
  Resume whatever pleaseth Thee;
Direct me as Thou wilt, I feel
  In every act Thou lovest me.

Oh, grant me but Thy love divine,
  My love for Thee will reign supreme;
Grant this, and all things else are mine,
  Without it life is but a dream.

C. C. Cox.

WHAT WENT YE OUT TO SEE?

WHAT went ye out to see
O'er the rude sandy lea,
Where stately Jordan flows by many a palm,
  Or where Gennesaret's wave
  Delights the flowers to lave
That o'er her western slope breathe airs of balm?

All through the summer night,
Those blossoms red and bright
Spread their soft breasts, unheeding, to the breeze.
Like hermits watching still
Around the sacred hill,
Where erst our Saviour watched upon His knees.

The Paschal moon above
Seems like a saint to rove,
Left shining in the world with Christ alone;
Below, the lake's still face
Sleeps sweetly in the embrace
Of mountains terraced high with mossy stone.

Here may we sit, and dream
Over the heavenly theme,
Till to our soul the former days return;
Till on the grassy bed, *
Where thousands once He fed,
The world's incarnate Maker we discern.

Oh, cross no more the main,
Wandering so wild and vain,
To count the reeds that tremble in the wind,
On listless dalliance bound,
Like children gazing round,
Who on God's works no seal of Godhead find:

Bask not in courtly bower,
Or sun-bright hall of power;
Pass Babel quick, and seek the holy land;

From robes of Tyrian dye
Turn with undazzled eye
To Bethlehem's glade, or Carmel's haunted strand.

Or choose thee out a cell
In Kedron's storied dell,
Beside the springs of Love, that never die:
Among the olives kneel
The chill night-blast to feel,
And watch the Moon that saw thy Master's agony.

Then rise at dawn of day
And wind thy thoughtful way
Where rested once the Temple's stately shade,
   With due feet tracing round
   The city's northern bound,
To th' other holy garden, where the Lord was laid.

   Who thus alternate see
   His death and victory,
Rising and falling as on angel wings,
   They, while they seem to roam,
   Draw daily nearer home,
Their heart untravelled still adores the King of kings.

   Or, if at home they stay,
   Yet are they, day by day,
In spirit journeying through the glorious land,
   Not for light Fancy's reed,
   Nor Honor's purple meed,
Nor gifted Prophet's lore, nor Science' wondrous wand.

   But more than Prophet, more
   Than Angels can adore
With face unveiled, is He they go to seek:
   Blessed be God, Whose grace
   Shows Him in every place
To homeliest hearts of pilgrims pure and meek!

KEBLE.

DOVE, LEAF, AND BOW.

Sweet Dove! the softest, steadiest plume
   In all the sunbright sky,
Brightening in ever-changeful bloom
   As breezes change on high;—

Sweet Leaf! the pledge of peace and mirth,
   "Long sought, and lately won,"
Blest increase of reviving Earth,
   When first it felt the Sun;—

Sweet Rainbow! pride of summer days,
   High set at Heaven's command,
Though into drear and dusky haze
   Thou melt on either hand;—

Dear tokens of a pardoning God,
   We hail ye, one and all,
As when our fathers walked abroad,
   Freed from their twelvemonth's thrall.

How joyful from the imprisoning ark
   On the green earth they spring!

Not blither, after showers, the Lark
　　Mounts up with glistening wing.

So home-bound sailors spring to shore.
　　Two oceans safely past;
So happy souls, when life is o'er,
　　Plunge in the empyreal vast.

What wins their first and fondest gaze
　　In all the blissful field,
And keeps it through a thousand days?
　　Love face to face revealed:

Love imaged in that cordial look
　　Our Lord in Eden bends
On souls that sin and earth forsook
　　In time to die · His friends.

And what most welcome and serene
　　Dawns on the Patriarch's eye,
In all the emerging hills so green,
　　In all the brightening sky?

What but the gentle rainbow's gleam,
　　Soothing the wearied sight,
That cannot bear the solar beam,
　　With soft undazzling light?

Lord, if our fathers turned to Thee
　　With such adoring gaze,

Wondering frail man Thy light should see
   Without Thy scorching blaze;

Where is our love, and where our hearts.
   We who have seen Thy Son,
Have tried Thy Spirit's winning arts.
   And yet we are not won?

The Son of God in radiance beamed
   Too bright for us to scan;
But we may face the rays that streamed
   From the mild Son of Man.

There, parted into rainbow hues,
   In sweet harmonious strife,
We see celestial love diffuse
   Its light o'er Jesus' life.

God, by His bow, vouchsafes to write
   This truth in Heaven above:
As every lovely hue is Light,
   So every grace is Love.

                   KEBLE.

MISSIONARY HYMN.

From Greenland's icy mountains,
 From India's coral strand,
Where Afric's sunny fountains
 Roll down their golden sand,
From many an ancient river,
 From many a palmy plain,
They call us to deliver
 Their land from error's chain.

What though the spicy breezes
  Blow soft o'er Ceylon's isle,
Though every prospect pleases,
  And only man is vile :
In vain with lavish kindness
  The gifts of God are strown;
The heathen in his blindness
  Bows down to wood and stone.

Can we, whose souls are lighted
  With wisdom from on high,
Can we to men benighted
  The lamp of life deny?
Salvation, oh, salvation,
  The joyful sound proclaim,
Till each remotest nation
  Has learned Messiah's name.

Waft, waft, ye winds. His story,
  And you, ye waters, roll,
Till like a sea of glory
  It spreads from pole to pole !
Till o'er our ransomed nature,
  The Lamb for sinners slain,
Redeemer, King, Creator,
  In bliss returns to reign !

                              HEBER.

EASTER EVEN.

REST of the weary! Thou
Thyself art resting now,
Where lowly in Thy sepulchre Thou liest;
From out her deathly sleep
My soul doth start, to weep
So sad a wonder, that Thou, Saviour, diest!

Thy bitter anguish o'er,
To this dark tomb they bore
Thee, Life of life—Thee, Lord of all creation!
The hollow rocky cave
Must serve Thee for a grave,
Who wast Thyself the Rock of our salvation.

O Prince of Life! I know
That when I too lie low,
Thou wilt at last my soul from death awaken:
Wherefore I will not shrink
From the grave's awful brink;
The heart that trusts in Thee shall ne'er be shaken.

To me the darksome tomb
Is but a narrow room,
Where I may rest in peace, from sorrow free.

Thy death shall give me power
To cry, in that dark hour,
O Death, O Grave, where is your victory?

The grave can naught destroy,
Only the flesh can die,
And e'en the body triumphs o'er decay:
Clothed by Thy wondrous might
In robes of dazzling light,
This flesh shall burst the grave at that last day.

My Jesus, day by day,
Help me to watch and pray
Beside the tomb where in my heart Thou'rt laid.
Thy bitter death shall be
My constant memory,
My guide at last into Death's awful shade.

FRANCK.

ADVENT SUNDAY.

AWAKE! again the Gospel trump is blown!
From year to year it swells with louder tone;
From year to year the signs of wrath
Are gathering round the Judge's path,
Strange words fulfilled, and mighty works achieved,
And truth in all the world both hated and believed.

Awake! why linger in the gorgeous town,
Sworn liegemen of the Cross and thorny crown?
Up from your beds of sloth, for shame,
Speed to the eastern mount like flame,
Nor wonder should ye find your King in tears,
Even with the loud Hosanna ringing in His ears.

Alas! no need to rouse them: long ago
They are gone forth to swell Messiah's show:
With glittering robes and garlands sweet
They strew the ground beneath His feet:
All but your hearts are there—O doomed to prove
The arrows winged in Heaven for Faith that will not love.

Meanwhile He paces through the adoring crowd,
Calm as the march of some majestic cloud,
That o'er wild scenes of ocean-war
Holds its still course in heaven afar:
Even so, heart-searching Lord, as years roll on,
Thou keepest silent watch from Thy triumphal throne:

Even so, the world is thronging round to gaze
On the dread vision of the latter days,
Constrained to own Thee, but in heart
Prepared to take Barabbas' part:
"Hosanna" now, to-morrow "Crucify,"
The changeful burden still of their rude lawless cry.

Yet in that throng of selfish hearts untrue
Thy sad eye rests upon Thy faithful few;

Children and childlike souls are there,
Blind Bartimeus' humble prayer,
And Lazarus wakened from his four days' sleep,
Enduring life again, that Passover to keep.

And first beside the olive-bordered way
Stands the blest home, where Jesus deigned to stay;
The peaceful home, to Zeal sincere
And heavenly Contemplation dear.

Where Martha loved to wait with reverence meet,
And wiser Mary lingered at Thy sacred feet.

Still through decaying ages as they glide,
Thou lov'st Thy chosen remnant to divide;
Sprinkled along the waste of years
Full many a soft green isle appears:
Pause where we may upon the desert road,
Some shelter is in sight, some sacred safe abode.

When withering blasts of error swept the sky,
And Love's last flower seemed fain to droop and die,
How sweet, how lone the ray benign
On sheltered nooks of Palestine!   .
Then to his early home did Love repair,
And cheered his sickening heart with his own native air.

Years roll away: again the tide of .crime
Has swept Thy footsteps from the favored clime.
Where shall the holy Cross find rest?
On a crowned monarch's mailéd breast:
Like some bright angel o'er the darkling scene,
Through court and camp he holds his heavenward course
        serene.

A fouler vision yet: an age of light,
Light without love, glares on the aching sight;
Oh, who can tell how calm and sweet,
Meek Walton, shows thy green retreat,
When, wearied with the tale thy times disclose,
The eye first finds thee out in thy secure repose?

Thus bad and good their several warnings give
Of His approach, whom none may see and live ;
Faith's ear, with awful still delight,
Counts them like minute-bells at night,
Keeping the heart awake till dawn of morn,
While to her funeral pile this aged world is borne.

But what are Heaven's alarms to hearts that cower
In wilful slumber, deepening every hour,
That draw their curtains closer round
The nearer swells the trumpet's sound ?
Lord, ere our trembling lamps sink down and die,
Touch us with chastening hand, and make us feel Thee nigh.

KEBLE.

THE PURIFICATION.

BLEST are the pure in heart,
For they shall see our God,
The secret of the Lord is theirs,
Their soul is Christ's abode.

Might mortal thought presume
To guess an angel's lay,
Such are the notes that echo through
The courts of Heaven to-day.

Such the triumphal hymns
On Sion's Prince that wait;
In high procession passing on
Towards His temple-gate.

Give ear, ye kings: bow down,
Ye rulers of the earth:
This, this is He; your Priest by grace,
Your God and King by birth.

No pomp of earthly guards
Attends with sword and spear,
And all-defying, dauntless look,
Their monarch's way to clear;

Yet are there more with Him
Than all that are with you,—
The armies of the highest Heaven,
All righteous, good, and true.

Spotless their robes and pure,
Dipped in the sea of light
That hides the unapproachéd shrine
From men's and angels' sight.

His throne thy bosom blest,
O Mother undefiled:
That throne, if aught beneath the skies,
Beseems the sinless child.

Lost in high thoughts, "whose son
The wondrous Babe might prove,"
Her guileless husband walks beside,
Bearing the hallowed dove :

Meet emblem of His vow
Who on this happy day
His dove-like soul—best sacrifice—
Did on God's altar lay.

But who is he, by years
Bowed, but erect in heart,
Whose prayers are struggling with his tears?
"Lord, let me now depart.

"Now hath Thy servant seen
Thy saving health, O Lord :
'Tis time that I depart in peace,
According to Thy word."

Yet swells the pomp : one more
Comes forth to bless her God :
Full fourscore years, meek widow, she
Her heavenward way hath trod.

She who to earthly joys
So long had given farewell
Now sees, unlooked for, Heaven on earth,
Christ in His Israel.

Wide open from that hour
The temple-gates are set,
And still the saints rejoicing there
The holy Child have met.

Now count His train to-day,
And who may meet Him, learn:
Him childlike sires, meek maidens, find,
Where pride can naught discern.

Still to the lowly soul
He doth Himself impart,
And for His cradle and His throne
Chooseth the pure in heart.

KEBLE.

WORK.

WHAT are we set on earth for? Say, to toil,
Nor seek to leave thy tending of the vines,
For all the heat o' the day, till it declines,
And Death's wild curfew shall from work assoil.
God did anoint thee with his odorous oil,
To wrestle, not to reign; and He assigns
All thy tears over, like pure crystallines,
For younger fellow-workers of the soil

To wear for amulets. So others shall
Take patience, labor, to their heart and hand,
From thy heart, and thy hand, and thy brave cheer,
And God's grace fructify through thee to all.
The least flower with a brimming cup may stand
And share its dew-drop with another near.

MRS. BROWNING.

THE STAR AND THE SCEPTRE.

Oh for a sculptor's hand,
   That thou mightst take thy stand,
Thy wild hair floating on the eastern breeze,
   Thy tranced yet open gaze
   Fixed on the desert haze,
As one who deep in heaven some airy pageant sees.

   In outline dim and vast
   Their fearful shadows cast
The giant forms of empires on their way
   To ruin: one by one
   They tower and they are gone;
Yet in the Prophet's soul the dreams of avarice stay.

   No sun or star so bright
   In all the world of light
That they should draw to Heaven his downward eye:
   He hears the Almighty's word,
   He sees the Angel's sword,
Yet low upon the earth his heart and treasure lie.

   Lo, from yon argent field,
   To him and us revealed,
One gentle Star glides down, on earth to dwell.

Chained as they are below,
Our eyes may see it glow,
And as it mounts again, may track its brightness well.

To him it glared afar,
A token of wild war,
The banner of his Lord's victorious wrath:
But close to us it gleams,
Its soothing lustre streams
Around our home's green walls, and on our churchway path.

We in the tents abide
Which he at distance eyed
Like goodly cedars by the waters spread.
While seven red altar-fires
Rose up in wavy spires,
Where on the mount he watched his sorceries dark and
dread.

He watched till morning's ray
On lake and meadow lay,
And willow-shaded streams, that silent sweep
Around the bannered lines,
Where by their several signs
The desert-wearied tribes in sight of Canaan sleep.

He watched till knowledge came
Upon his soul like flame,
Not of those magic fires at random caught;
But true Prophetic light
Flashed o'er him, high and bright,
Flashed once, and died away, and left his darkened thought.

57

And can he choose but fear
Who feels his God so near
That, when he fain would curse, his powerless tongue
In blessing only moves?
Alas! the world he loves
Too close around his heart her tangling veil hath flung.

Sceptre and Star divine,
Who in Thine inmost shrine
Hast made us worshippers, oh, claim Thine own;
More than Thy seers we know:
Oh, teach our love to grow
Up to Thy heavenly light, and reap what Thou hast sown.

KEBLE.

WHITSUNDAY.

WHEN God of old came down from Heaven,
In power and wrath He came;
Before His feet the clouds were riven,
Half darkness and half flame.

Around the trembling mountain's base
The prostrate people lay;
A day of wrath, and not of grace,—
A dim and dreadful day.

But when He came the second time,
  He came in power and love;
Softer than gale at morning prime
  Hovered His holy Dove.

The fires that rushed on Sinai down
  In sudden torrents dread,
Now gently light, a glorious crown,
  On every sainted head.

Like arrows went those lightnings forth,
  Winged with the sinner's doom,
But these, like tongues, o'er all the earth
  Proclaiming life to come:

And as on Israel's awe-struck ear
  The voice exceeding loud,
The trump, that angels quake to hear,
  Thrilled from the deep, dark cloud;

So when the Spirit of our God
  Came down His flock to find,
A voice from Heaven was heard abroad,
  A rushing, mighty wind.

Nor doth the outward ear alone
  At that high warning start:
Conscience gives back the appalling tone;
  'Tis echoed in the heart.

It fills the Church of God ; it fills
  The sinful world around ;
Only in stubborn hearts and wills
  No place for it is found.

To other strains our souls are set ;
  A giddy whirl of sin
Fills ear and brain, and will not let
  Heaven's harmonies come in.

Come Lord, come Wisdom, Love, and Power,
  Open our ears to hear ;
Let us not miss the accepted hour.
  Save, Lord, by Love or Fear.

KEBLE.

JOY IN HEAVEN.

THERE was joy in Heaven !
There was joy in Heaven !
When this goodly world to frame
The Lord of might and mercy came :
Shouts of joy were heard on high,
And the stars sang from the sky,
  "Glory to God in Heaven !"

There was joy in Heaven!
There was joy in Heaven!
When the billows. heaving dark.
Sank around the stranded ark.
And the rainbow's watery span
Spake of mercy, hope to man,
   And peace with God in Heaven!

There was joy in Heaven!
There was joy in Heaven!
When of love the midnight beam
Dawned on the towers of Bethlehem;
And along the echoing hill
Angels sang, "On earth good will,
   And glory in the Heaven!"

There is joy in Heaven!
There is joy in Heaven!
When the sheep that went astray
Turns again to virtue's way;
When the soul. by grace subdued,
Sobs its prayer of gratitude,
   Then is there joy in Heaven!

               HEBER.

THE LILIES.

Sweet nurslings of the vernal skies,
    Bathed in soft airs, and fed with dew,
What more than magic in you lies,
    To fill the heart's fond view?
In childhood's sports, companions gay,
In sorrow, on Life's downward way,
How soothing! in our last decay
    Memorials prompt and true.

Relics ye are of Eden's bowers,
    As pure, as fragrant, and as fair
As when ye crowned the sunshine hours
    Of happy wanderers there.
Fallen all beside,—the world of life,
How is it stained with fear and strife!
In Reason's world what storms are rife,
    What passions range and glare!

But cheerful and unchanged the while
    Your first and perfect form ye show,
The same that won Eve's matron smile
    In the world's opening glow.

The stars of heaven a course are taught
Too high above our human thought;
Ye may be found if ye are sought,
   And as we gaze, we know.

Ye dwell beside our paths and homes,
   Our paths of sin, our homes of sorrow.
And guilty man, where'er he roams,
   Your innocent mirth may borrow.
The birds of air before us fleet,
They cannot brook our shame to meet;
But we may taste your solace sweet
   And come again to-morrow.

Ye fearless in your nests abide;
   Nor may we scorn, too proudly wise,
Your silent lessons, undescried
   By all but lowly eyes;
For ye could draw the admiring gaze
Of Him who worlds and hearts surveys;
Your order wild, your fragrant maze,
   He taught us how to prize.

Ye felt your Maker's smile that hour,
   As when he paused and owned you good;
His blessing on earth's primal bower,
   Ye felt it all renewed.
What care ye now, if winter's storm
Sweep ruthless o'er each silken form?
Christ's blessing at your heart is warm,
   Ye fear no vexing mood.

Alas! of thousand bosoms kind,
  That daily court you and caress,
How few the happy secret find
  Of your calm loveliness!
"Live for to-day! to-morrow's light
To-morrow's cares shall bring to sight;
Go sleep like closing flowers at night,
  And Heaven thy morn will bless."

KEBLE.

ST. STEPHEN.

THE Son of God goes forth to war,
  A kingly crown to gain :
His blood-red banner streams afar :
  Who follows in His train ?

Who best can drink his cup of woe,
  Triumphant over pain,
Who patient bears his cross below,
  He follows in His train !

The martyr first, whose eagle eye
  Could pierce beyond the grave ;
Who saw his Master in the sky,
  And called on Him to save.

Like Him, with pardon on his tongue
  In midst of mortal pain,
He prayed for them that did the wrong !
  Who follows in his train ?

A glorious band, the chosen few
  On whom the Spirit came ;
Twelve valiant saints, their hope they knew.
  And mocked the cross and flame.

59

They met the tyrant's brandished steel,
  The lion's gory mane;
They bowed their necks the death to feel!
  Who follows in their train?

A noble army,—men and boys,
  The matron and the maid,
Around the Saviour's throne rejoice,
  In robes of light arrayed.

They climbed the steep ascent of Heaven,
  Through peril, toil, and pain!
O God, to us may grace be given
  To follow in their train!

HEBER.

PRAYER AT THE POLE.

A LITTLE group of worn-out men,
  With weary limbs and shattered forms,
Whose stalwart wills and gallant hearts
  Were strong to face dark danger's storms!
And one amidst them, slight of frame,
  And pale from strife with death and pain,

A hero's soul, whose martyr zeal
   Bore nobly suffering's cankering chain

They met within the solemn aisles
   Of ice-built shrine, a temple grand,
Alone upon a frozen sea,
   The saving and the rescued band,
Mid crystal columns reared aloft
   Against a gray and cloud-draped dome,—

The only thing—that shadowed sky—
    In all the waste that looked like home!

They stood with bowed, uncovered heads,
    With reverent mien and moistened eyes,
Remembering scenes that long had passed,
    Recalling love's most tender ties,
As softly on the keen, cold air
    Their leader's voice rose calm and clear,
And raised, like prophet's tone, the hope
    That in each heart had found a bier.

Few words of humble, grateful praise,
    For guidance, life, and rest, a prayer,
A low "Amen" from quivering lips,
    Were all the pomps of service there!
It gave them strength to conquer death;
    It made them brave to dare and do;
It kept them faithful to the end,
    A band of brothers, tried and true!

Then bless them, souls of Christian men
    O'er all the earth who praise and pray:
And bless him most of all, their chief,
    Who first in duty led the way,—
Who first upon those regions drear
    Of frozen, unknown waters spoke
The name of Christ, whose world-blest sound
    The solitude of silence broke!

Those polar mounts of ice may melt
    Beneath the Arctic's summer skies;

May speed the nations' hoarded wealth,
   And 'neath the tropics ebb and rise ;
Yet bear abroad, where'er they flow,
   That baptism of the holy Name
They echoed from his voice who died
   And left those bergs to spread his fame !

SALLIE BRIDGES.

ST. AGNES' EVE.

DEEP on the convent-roof the snows
   Are sparkling to the moon :
My breath to heaven like vapor goes :
   May my soul follow soon !
The shadows of the convent-towers
   Slant down the snowy sward,
Still creeping with the creeping hours
   That lead me to my Lord :
Make Thou my spirit pure and clear
   As are the frosty skies,
Or this first snowdrop of the year
   That in my bosom lies.

As these white robes are soiled and dark,
   To yonder shining ground ;

As this pale taper's earthly spark,
   To yonder argent round;
So shows my soul before the Lamb,
   My spirit before Thee;
So in mine earthly house I am,
   To that I hope to be.
Break up the heavens, O Lord, and far,
   Through all yon starlight keen,
Draw me, Thy bride, a glittering star,
   In raiment white and clean.

He lifts me to the golden doors;
   The flashes come and go;
All Heaven bursts her starry floors,
   And strews her lights below.
And deepens on and up! the gates
   Roll back, and far within
For me the heavenly Bridegroom waits,
   To make me pure of sin.
The sabbaths of Eternity,
   One sabbath deep and wide;
A light upon the shining sea,—
   The Bridegroom with His bride!

TENNYSON.

PRAISE.

Praise the Lord!
Praise Him from the heavens on high!
Praise Him in the lofty sky!
Praise Him, all ye angels bright!
Praise Him, all His hosts of light!
Praise Him, sun and moon afar!
Praise Him, every radiant star!

Praise Him, heavens that heavens upbear;
Waters, higher hung in air;
Let them praise their Maker's name;
For He called them, and they came:
He has fixed their places fast,
With a bound which ne'er was passed.

Praise the Lord from earth below,
Monsters, through the deep that go:
Fire, and cloud, and snow, and hail,
And the obedient stormy gale;
Mountains, and the highlands all,
Fruitful trees, and cedars tall:

Beasts that field or forest bore ;
Worms that creep, and birds that soar ;
Kings. and men of humble birth ;
Princes, judges of the earth ;
Youths and virgins, flourishing
In the beauty of your spring ;

You who bow with age's weight,
You who were but born of late ;
Heaven and earth with due consent,
Praise His name most excellent ;
He His saints to Him shall rear,
Israel, to the Lord so dear.
          Praise the Lord !

THE HOLY SEPULCHRE.

THEN hallowed peace renewed her wealthy reign,
Then altars smoked, and Sion smiled again.
There sculptured gold and costly gems were seen,
And all the bounties of the British queen ;
There barbarous kings their sandalled nations led,
And steel-clad champions bowed the crested head.
There, when her fiery race the desert poured,
And pale Byzantium feared Medina's sword,
When coward Asia shook in trembling woe,
And bent appalled before the Bactrian bow ;
From the moist regions of the western star
The wandering hermit waked the storm of war.

Their limbs all iron, and their souls all flame,
A countless host, the red-cross warriors came.

E'en hoary priests the sacred combat wage,
And clothe in steel the palsied arm of age;
While beardless youths and tender maids assume
The weighty morion and the glancing plume.
In sportive pride the warrior damsels wield
The ponderous falchion, and the sun-like shield,
And start to see their armor's iron gleam
Dance with blue lustre in Tabaria's stream.

The blood-red banner floating o'er their van,
All madly blithe the mingled myriads ran:
Impatient Death beheld his destined food,
And hovering vultures snuffed the scent of blood.

*   *   *

*   *

Yet still destruction sweeps the lonely plain,
And heroes lift the generous sword in vain.
Still o'er her sky the clouds of anger roll,
And God's revenge hangs heavy on her soul.
Yet shall she rise,—but not by war restored,
Not built in murder,—planted by the sword:
Yes, Salem, thou shalt rise: thy Father's aid
Shall heal the wound His chastening hand has made:
Shall judge the proud oppressor's ruthless sway,
And burst his brazen bonds, and cast his cords away.
Then on your tops shall deathless verdure spring,
Break forth, ye mountains, and ye valleys, sing!
No more your thirsty rocks shall frown forlorn,
The unbeliever's jest, the heathen's scorn,

The sultry sands shall tenfold harvest yield,
And a new Eden deck the thorny field.
E'en now, perchance, wide-waving o'er the land,
That mighty angel lifts his golden wand,
Courts the bright vision of descending power,
Tells every gate, and measures every tower;
And chides the tardy seals that yet detain
Thy Lion, Judah, from His destined reign.

And who is He? the vast, the awful form,
Girt with the whirlwind, sandalled with the storm?
A western cloud around His limbs is spread,
His crown a rainbow, and a sun His head.
To highest Heaven He lifts His kingly hand,
And treads at once the ocean and the land;
And, hark! His voice amid the thunder's roar,
His dreadful voice, that time shall be no more!

.

Lo! cherub hands the golden courts prepare,
Lo! thrones arise, and every saint is there;
Earth's utmost bounds confess their awful sway,
The mountains worship, and the isles obey;
Nor sun nor moon they need,—nor day, nor night;—
God is their temple, and the Lamb their light:
And shall not Israel's sons exulting come,
Hail the glad beam, and claim their ancient home?
On David's throne shall David's offspring reign,
And the dry bones be warm with life again.
Hark! white-robed crowds their deep hosannas raise,
And the hoarse flood repeats the sound of praise;

Ten thousand harps attune the mystic song,
Ten thousand thousand saints the strain prolong;
" Worthy the Lamb! omnipotent to save,
Who .died, who lives, triumphant o'er the grave !"

HEBER.

PARVUM QUANDO CERNO DEUM.

WHEN within His mother's arms
  I the infant God behold,
All my heart the vision warms
  With a blessedness untold.

Leaps He, mother, leaps the boy,
  Gazing at thy holy breast;
Kisses with a smile of joy,
  Thousand kisses, fondly prest!

As upon the stainless skies
  Peaceful hangs the new-born sun,
So upon thy bosom lies,
  Mother pure, thy Holy One.

Ah! how lovely that repose!
  Mother with the infant fair;
Twined as with the tender rose
  Violet and lily are.

Many a silent clasp of bliss,
　　Many a look of smiling love;
As the flowers the meadow kiss,
　　As the starry eyes above.

Oh, if one such loving dart,
　　Falling on that mother mild,
May but fall upon my heart,
　　Infant Jesus, Holy Child!

WASHBURN.

CHRIST RISEN.

CHRIST rises; lightning-stricken at the sight,
　　The arméd soldiery, who at the tomb
　　Kept their unholy watch, and walked the gloom,
Fall back, their faces hid in dread affright,
And like the scared shadows of the night
　　Hasten away; as when the aerial dome
　　The rising moon doth suddenly illume,
With silent intervention calm and bright
　　Just rising, and the clouds departing fly,
And flying feebly catch her silver ray.
　　E'en so those heathen thoughts which held their sway
And ever in the heart were hiding nigh,

When Christ doth visit us, before His way
Shall flee, and He shall fill the untroubled sky.

Christ rises! not alone, with Him His own
   Are rising from their graves, and burst the veil,
   And look again on this their earthly jail,
E'en as the moon doth not arise alone,
But watchful sentinels attend her throne,
   Yet love that they themselves should fade and fail,
   In her surpassing lustre dim and pale.
'Tis thus when Christ within the soul made known
   His glorious resurrection shall declare,
His love and light shall dissipate the gloom;
Nor shall He thither unattended come,
But all the graces with Him make their home,
   When He the darkness of the soul lays bare,
   Fain to vouchsafe His gracious presence there.

THE REAPERS' RETURN HOME.

Through the golden tints of sunset,
   'Neath the glowing, crimsoned skies,
With each smiling face uplifted,
   Where their work's warm flush still lies,
All the reapers, homeward going.
   In a happy, cheerful throng,

With gay voices sing the chorus
  Of an olden harvest-song.

They have mowed the waving glory
  Of the ripe and bending grain.
Have knelt down where summer's splendor
  Mid the aisle of sheaves has lain,
And have gathered up the richness
  Of the small seed sown before,

Then with glad eyes stood rejoicing
In the sure and garnered store.

Now they onward walk together
Through the green and pleasant field.
And each worker, like a sceptre,
His sharp, shining scythe doth wield;
While the matrons toss their infants
To the measure of the tune,
Maidens, wishing o'er their shoulders,
Watch the dim, new-rising moon.

There are glances shy and tender
Under manly, sunburned brows;
There are blushings at bold whispers,
And fresh murmurs of old vows;
There are laughters free and ringing,
Plucking flowers by the way,
And fond clinging of hands parted
By their labor all the day.

Age and youth and careless childhood
Share the music of the strain.
As they wend through clover fragrance
Towards their waiting homes again.
Where the night unto the weary
Will give slumber without dreams,
And bring silence with deep shadows,
Till another morning beams.

There is reaping, there is gathering
For us all upon the earth,

And the sheaves we show at harvest
　Are what prove each spirit's worth !
Let us do our work so bravely
　That our hearts shall sing with praise
In the glow of heaven's glory
　At the closing of our days !
When we lie down for our resting
　In our last home dark and still,
May each tried soul find its waking
　Where Truth's rays the mansions fill !

SALLIE BRIDGES.

THE RETURN HOME.

SAFE home, safe home in port !
　Rent cordage, shattered deck,
Torn sails, provisions short,
　And only not a wreck :
But, oh, the joy upon the shore
To tell our voyage-perils o'er !

The prize, the prize secure !
　The athlete nearly fell :
Bare all he could endure,
　And bare not always well :

63

But he may smile at troubles gone
Who sets the victor's garland on!

No more the foe can harm:
  No more of leaguered camp,
And cry of night-alarm,
  And need of ready lamp:
And yet how nearly he had failed,—
How nearly had that foe prevailed!

The lamb is in the fold
  In perfect safety penned:
The lion once had hold,
  And thought to make an end.
But One came by with wounded side,
And for the sheep the Shepherd died.

The exile is at home!
  Oh, nights and days of tears,

Oh, longings not to roam,
   Oh, sins, and doubts, and fears!
What matter now, when (so men say)
The King has wiped those tears away?

O happy, happy Bride.
   Thy widowed hours are past,
The Bridegroom at thy side,
   Thou all His Own at last!
The sorrows of thy former cup
In full fruition swallowed up!

St. Joseph of the Studium.

Lord, what a change within us one short hour
Spent in Thy presence will prevail to make!
What heavy burdens from our bosoms take,
What parchéd grounds refresh, as with a shower!
We kneel, and all around us seems to lower;
We rise, and all, the distant and the near,
Stands forth in sunny outline, brave and clear;
We kneel how weak, we rise how full of power!
Why, therefore, should we do ourselves this wrong,
Or others,—that we are not always strong;
That we are ever overborne with care;
That we should ever weak or heartless be,
Anxious or troubled, when with us in prayer,
And joy, and strength, and courage, are with Thee?

Trench.

ALTITUDO, QUID HIC JACES?

Height of heaven, why art Thou lying
   Cradled in a stable base?
Maker of the starry torches,
   Hides a manger cold Thy face?

Oh, what marvels hast Thou lavished,
  Jesu, upon sinful men!
Exiles from the bliss of Eden,
  Yet Thy heart hath loved again.

Might divine becometh weakness;
  Infinite a babe could be;
In a mortal womb imprisoned,
  Born——behold Eternity!
Oh, what marvels hast Thou lavished,
  Jesu, upon sinful men!
Exiles from the bliss of Eden,
  Yet Thy heart hath loved again.

Thou with childish lips wast clinging
  To the stainless Virgin's breast;
Tear-drops from Thine eye were springing,—
  Thou, the Joy of heaven blest!
Oh, what marvels hast Thou lavished,
  Jesu, upon sinful men!
Exiles from the bliss of Eden,
  Yet Thy heart hath loved again.

WASHBURN.

THE PRODIGAL.

Why feedest thou on husks so coarse and rude?
I could not be content with angels' food.

How camest thou companion to the swine?
I loathed the courts of heaven, the choir divine.

Who bade thee crouch in hovel dark and drear?
I left a palace wide to sojourn here.

Harsh tyrant's slave who made thee, once so free?
A father's rule too heavy seemed to me.

What sordid rags hang round thee on the breeze?
I laid immortal robes aside for these.

An exile through the world who bade thee roam?
None; but I wearied of a happy home.

Why must thou dweller in a desert be?
A garden seemed not fair enough to me.

Why sue a beggar at the mean world's door?
To live on God's large bounty seemed so poor.

What has thy forehead so to earthward brought?
To lift it higher than the stars I thought.

TRENCH.

LUCIS LARGITOR SPLENDIDE.

MATIN HYMN OF ST. AMBROSE, FOURTH CENTURY.

ALL GLORIOUS Giver of the light,
 In Whose unclouded ray,
After the shadows of the night,
 Blooms the new-risen day!

Thou art the world's true morning star;
 Not he, that lesser one,
Twinkling a feeble speck afar,
 Pale herald of the sun.

O brighter than the noontide gleam;
   Day, sun full-orbed Thou art,
Piercing with Thine eternal beam
   The cloisters of the heart.

Builder of living worlds, draw nigh!
   Smile of the Father's face!
Our happy souls wide open lie
   To Thy soft-coming grace.

Filled with Thy Spirit, may we keep
   God's presence aye within;
Nor through these hallowed portals creep
   The stealthy feet of sin.

Amid thick-coming cares, that fill
   The hours of daily time,
Our law shall be Thy perfect will,
   Our conscience clear of crime!

With virgin shame may the chaste mind
   Our earth-born passions chain,
And in this body pure enshrined
   Thy Holy Ghost remain.

Be this glad hope our matin song,
   This, Lord, our sacrifice!
O morning light, through midnight long
   Watch with unsleeping eyes!

WASHBURN.

John Keble.

NATURE AND GRACE.

THERE is a book, who runs may read,
 Which heavenly truth imparts,
And all the lore its scholars need,
 Pure eyes and Christian hearts.

The works of God above, below.
 Within us, and around,

Are pages in that book, to show
  How God Himself is found.

The glorious sky embracing all
  Is like the Maker's love,
Wherewith encompassed, great and small
  In peace and order move.

The Moon above, the Church below,
  A wondrous race they run;
But all their radiance, all their glow,
  Each borrows of its Sun.

The Saviour lends the light and heat
  That crowns His holy hill;
The saints, like stars, around His seat
  Perform their courses still.

The saints above are stars in Heaven:
  What are the saints on earth?
Like trees they stand whom God has given,
  Our Eden's happy birth.

Faith is their fixed unswerving root,
  Hope their unfading flower,
Fair deeds of charity their fruit,
  The glory of their bower.

The dew of Heaven is like Thy grace,
  It steals in silence down;

But where it lights, the favored place
  By richest fruits is known.

One Name above all glorious names,
  With its ten thousand tongues,
The everlasting sea proclaims,
  Echoing angelic songs.

The raging Fire, the roaring Wind,
  Thy boundless power display:
But in the gentler breeze we find
  Thy Spirit's viewless way.

Two worlds are ours: 'tis only Sin
  Forbids us to descry
The mystic heaven and earth within,
  Plain as the sea and sky.

Thou, who hast given me eyes to see
  And love this sight so fair,
Give me a heart to find out Thee
  And read Thee everywhere.

KEBLE.

RECORDARE SANCTÆ CRUCIS.

BONAVENTURA, THIRTEENTH CENTURY.

PONDER thou the cross all-holy,
Who wilt tread the pathway lowly
 To the perfect joy above:
Thou the holy cross aye ponder,
And, with an uncloying wonder,
 Drink its mysteries of love.

When thou toilest, when thou sleepest,
When thou smilest, when thou weepest,
 Sad or gladsome if thou art,
In thy coming, in thy going,
Whether pain or solace knowing,
 Keep the cross within thy heart.

In the cross, mid burdens aching,
Heaviest waves above thee breaking,
 Thine unending comfort find:

Though midst cruel foes thou languish,
Sweet the cross in every anguish,
   Refuge of the pious mind.

Cross, of Paradise the portal,
Where have clung the souls immortal,
   Victors in this earthly strife;
Holy cross, the whole world's healing;
By it is God's love revealing
   Marvels of eternal life.

Cross of Christ, the soul's well being,
Light unshadowed for our seeing,
   For the heart its sweetest good;
Cross, the life all saints indwelling,
Storehouse of all gifts excelling,
   Beauty and beatitude.

Cross, the glass of brave endeavor;
Leader of our triumph ever;
   Hope the faithful to inspire;
Badge of the elect of heaven;
Succor in our trial given;
   Fulness of the soul's desire.

Cross, the tree in beauty growing,
Hallowed by Christ's life-blood flowing,
   Hanging with full-ripened load;
Bounty for all spirits bearing,
An immortal banquet sharing
   With the blessed sons of God.

Crucified, oh, make me stronger,
While my life is spared me longer,
  Still to know Thy suffering;
With Thee wounded, with Thee dying,
To that Form before me lying
  On the holy cross I cling.

WASHBURN.

ALL ANGELS.

THOMAS A KEMPIS, FOURTEENTH CENTURY.

EVER stand the angel throng,
Lauding God in holy song;
Gazing on their glorious King,
With the heart, the voice they sing;
Harp-notes flinging, timbrels ringing,
Now on golden plumes upspringing,
Climbing on the heavenly stair;
Sweet bells blending, white-robed bending
Near the highest Trinity;
Holy, Holy, Holy, crying:
Flieth sorrow, ceaseth sighing.
In that city of the sky.

Mingled are all happy voices,
One that in their God rejoices;
Love in every mind is burning,
In pure vision upward turning
To the Eternal One, the Blessed Trine.
All the glowing seraphim
With a heart of fire adore Him;
All the keen-eyed cherubim
Veil their faces low before Him:
Awed the Thrones behold the Majesty divine.

Oh, how wonderful that region!
Oh, how beautiful that legion!
Men with angels ever bright!
Shining city, aye in thee
Reigneth full tranquillity,—
In thy borders peace and light.
Dwellers of this city fair
Garments white of chasteness wear;
In one household of sweet love,
One unbroken circle move.
Naught of darkness, naught of care,
Grief, temptation, haunteth there:
Free from sickness, ever blest,
Theirs of every good the best.

WASHBURN.

THE END.

www.ingramcontent.com/pod-product-compliance
Lightning Source LLC
Chambersburg PA
CBHW030638030726
47497CB00006B/1848